RELIEF FROM STUTTERING

*Laying the Groundwork to Speak
with Greater Ease*

Papers and Commentary

ELLEN-MARIE SILVERMAN

ISBN-10: 1482084759
EAN-13: 9781482084757

Library of Congress Control Number: 2013901791
CreateSpace Independent Publishing Platform
North Charleston, South Carolina

For those I have known who have been on the journey and
For those of us on our way

Perhaps, the most novel and, consequently, most provocative message is that those of us with stuttering problems are fundamentally the same as everyone else. We share far more similarities than differences in outlook and drive. We all desire to be happy and do whatever we can to be so. We all fear rejection and abandonment and do what we know to feel safe. Clinging to a false, divisive notion that we are outsiders, alien from those without stuttering problems, for which there is only evidence to the contrary, creates a membrane of fear that can encompass us and soften our decision and resolve to change and invite family members, acquaintances, and strangers to relate to us with sympathy that reduces expectations for us rather than with compassion in recognition of our shared humanity that encourages us to be all that we are.

– – – From *Relief From Stuttering*

Other Books by Ellen-Marie Silverman

Fiction

JASON'S SECRET

Non-Fiction

MIND MATTERS
MINDFULNESS & STUTTERING

Contents

FOREWORD: WINGS

But don't be satisfied with stories,
How things have gone with others. Unfold
Your own myth, without complicated explanation . . .
Your legs will get heavy and tired. Then comes a moment
Of feeling the wings you've grown,
Lifting . . .
--- Rumi, *et al.*, "Unfold Your Own Myth," 2004, p. 40

On the surface, *Relief From Stuttering* is a story of how one woman found relief from the pain and struggle of stuttering. This story of her lived experience with stuttering has appeal for people who stutter, family and friends of people who stutter, and speech-language pathologists. As a speech-language pathologist who has worked with people who stutter for almost 30 years, this book offered me a deeper understanding of the inner experiences of some of my clients and greater insight into how I may help them find relief from their struggles.

Down deep, this book is a microcosm of the universal human story to overcome suffering and find happiness. The universal nature of Dr. Ellen-Marie Silverman's story broadens its appeal beyond those affiliated with stuttering to all those wanting relief from any kind of struggle. Ellen trusted stuttering to be her teacher, and she became its disciple. The Master Teacher of Stuttering led her through the human wounds of fear, inadequacy, and shame, to her higher self -- a self of non-judgment, compassion, and abundant kindness.

In these essays and commentaries, Ellen tells her story, without complicated explanation, of the sometimes daunting work of breaking old cycles of reflexive response in order to experience the ultimate blessing of freedom. Not freedom as in stutter-free or pain-free, but a more powerful freedom to choose her own attitude toward her circumstances and freedom to accept herself as is --- existential freedom. We all want to be free of suffering and to have happiness. Most of us have wounds that pain us so deeply we can't bear to uncover them and look at them for very long. Ellen found the courage to look, and through intentional daily practice, she transcended the pain of her stuttering and became her true self.

But Ellen doesn't ask us to be satisfied with reading the story of how things went with her. Our wings don't lift us up until our legs have grown too tired and heavy to move; the blessing doesn't enfold us until we've wrestled all night with the angel, as the Biblical story of Jacob tells us. Wings and blessings only grace us when we have done the hard work on ourselves, and only under conditions of non-judgment and compassion. Her gift, wrapped in these essays, is the story of how we each must do our own difficult work, feeling our legs grow heavy and tired, until we eventually feel our wings lifting us up. Each of us has this capacity within ourselves. Ellen-Marie Silverman's story gives us the gift of possibilities.

Cindy S. Spillers, Ph. D.
March, 2013

LAYING THE GROUNDWORK: AN ORIENTATION

This is a book I never intended to write. It simply evolved as a statement of what I believe is required when embarking on a path of change from being a person with a stuttering problem to being someone who may stutter now and then and what provides support along the way.

HOW THIS BOOK CAME TO BE

The book consists of 12 papers I presented at International Stuttering Awareness Day (ISAD) Online Conferences from 2000 to 2012 with added commentary for each that I wrote especially for this book. The Conference for people with stuttering problems, students, professionals, and the general public alike encouraged sharing of information and concerns about the nature and treatment of stuttering problems. When I learned that the facility that had been archiving and making Conference content available online may stop doing so, I decided to fashion the papers I wrote, for which I hold the copyright, into a book for a readership identical in composition to that of conference attendees, namely, people with stuttering problems, professionals, and those seeking to better understand stuttering problems and ways to help themselves or others who have stuttering problems speak more as they wish. It is my intent and hope that those who may find these papers helpful continue to have access to them.

I have included all 12 papers which I edited slightly to conform to a book presentation by eliminating introductory remarks suited only to conference delivery and by adding or removing content to resolve potential ambiguity or to eliminate redundancy. Otherwise, each is as originally presented. They appear in chronological order, from the first, "*Jason's Secret*: What It Feels Like to Stutter," presented in 2000, to the most recent, "Why Seek Therapy," presented in 2012, skipping the year 2002, when I did not contribute a paper to the Conference.

Some attending these online conferences posted requests in the threaded discussion sections linked to each paper for additional information or for specific advice about applying the suggestions the papers offered. Such feedback, not at all unexpected and welcomed from engaged readers, often identified a need for elaboration the 2,000 word per paper limit had made impossible. Their feedback prompted me to write a commentary for each for this book. Written during the last half of 2012, the commentaries lightly expand on aspects of the papers I consider most practical, most provocative, or both. So, my intention to keep the essays available and to amplify their usefulness was the genesis of this book. My overarching goal: To finish the work I started by emphasizing that replacing out-worn, unhelpful beliefs and behaviors with healthy ones leads us to speak more as we wish, if that is our desire, and that "Know thyself" may be our most practical practice and goal, as ancient Greek seers advised.

CHANGING TO SPEAK MORE AS WE WISH

When I began consciously formulating this book, I had presented a total of nine papers addressing, in one way or another, the theme of changing from being a person with a stuttering problem to being someone who may stutter now and then but who no longer has a stuttering problem, a journey I myself have been on. I knew the suggestions contained in these essays drawn from my academic knowledge of stuttering and stuttering problems, work as a clinical and research speech pathologist, and personal journey to speak with greater ease could help lay the groundwork for satisfy-ing exchanges between clients and clinicians and for the thoughtful selection and skillful application of congenial and satisfying self-help practices by those working on their own. Although I wrote the papers with no intention of formulating an exposition of what is required and what is involved in the change process, I knew by the time I considered writing the tenth that that was what I had been doing and what I intended to continue doing. I recognized that, individually and collectively, the papers underscore the reality that *we live what we believe*, a belief I firmly hold and a topic, until then, in my experience, rarely considered in a public forum devoted to stuttering problems. So, in the final three papers, I continued to address that theme and its corollary, namely, that by getting to know ever more deeply what we believe, we become better able and more likely to do what we need to do to speak and to live as we wish.

Perhaps, the most novel and, consequently, the most provoca-tive message of the collection is that those of us with stuttering problems are fundamentally the same as everyone else. We share far more similarities than differences in outlook and drive. We *all* desire to be happy and do whatever we can to be so, and we *all* fear rejection and abandonment and do what we know to feel safe. Clinging to a false, unhelpful notion that we are outsiders, alien from those without stuttering problems, for which there is only con-siderable evidence to the contrary, encourages us to generate a membrane of fear that can encompass us, softening our decision and resolve to change and invite family members, acquaintances, and strangers to relate to us with sympathy that reduces expecta-tions for us rather than with compassion in recognition of our shared humanity that encourages us to be all that we are.

My re-reading of the collection suggested that individually and collectively they are riffs on four fundamental themes: Honoring Self-Worth, Fearlessly Facing Fear, Charting A Path Of Change, and Using Helpful Assessment Metrics.

Honoring Self-Worth

To change as we wish, applying whatever methods we find agreeable, *we need first and foremost to believe we are worthy of change.* The Declaration of Independence of the United States of America proclaims we all are endowed with ". . . certain unalienable rights . . ." among which is " . . . the pursuit of happiness . . ." Yet many of us who live under this doctrine believe that, although collectively we have the right to pursue happiness, personally we do not deserve to be happy if we look or act differently from family, culture, or societal expectations. This inherently false notion fuels targeted and financially successful business practices which capitalize on our fear of rejection. We who live in the West and in western influenced societies find it difficult to evade advertisements in all forms of media and on the internet that encourage us to purchase hair replacement products and services, fitness regimes that sculpt our abs and firm our buttocks, elective surgery to hide signs we are aging, stuttering help, and so forth to be acceptable and accepted. We may find it even more difficult to ignore their implicit and false message that we can not be happy unless we look, speak, and live like the people populating the ads. But we can. So the first requisite for speaking with greater ease becomes that of seeing ourselves *as we are* as worthy of seeking and experiencing greater happiness.

Then *we need to believe there is a way or ways for us to speak more as we wish and to do so more consistently.* Locating potential options is the easy part. An online search can quickly locate scholarly papers, accessible books, programs, and other means supposedly helpful to those of us wishing to resolve our stuttering problems. But making practical use of this information is not often easy or possible. New research findings describing group tendencies often translate poorly or not at all to personal need and application. And what helped someone else, "personality" or not, may not help us. But no method, no technique, no pharmaceutical, and no device will help us unless we want to change, consider ourselves worthy of change, believe we can change, find a way to change, *and, then, change.*

To change, we need to know what we really want and what we really believe about ourselves. If we do not take time to discover our deepest desires and beliefs, our effort may be perfunctory rather than whole-hearted and our results less than what we hoped and, even more distressing, likely to strengthen the doubt we already may carry that, maybe, speaking as we wish more consistently is not something we can do. For most of us, the critical task becomes that of looking inward, but it is one we often tell ourselves is expendable because we do not want to experience the self-loathing we fear we may feel for having a stuttering problem we have yet to resolve. So we rationalize: We tell ourselves we do not need to spend time in self-analysis. We only need to locate and employ the right tools to speak as we wish.

This falsehood, appealing to our desire to avoid pain, resembles the misdirection we can give ourselves if we contemplate shedding excess weight. Wanting to weigh less, we can tell ourselves that all we need to do is to put ourselves on the right diet, a strategy I and countless others know rarely works in the long-term and, sometimes, not even in the short-term. Adopting such a plan, we may quit before we lose our goal weight. We find faithfully following diets, especially those directing us to consume meals consisting primarily of single foods, such as watermelon, cabbage soup, and animal protein, too punitive, too boring, or too unappealing, especially if we fail to experience the loss of poundage we desire as quickly as we wish. And if we do follow a diet until we lose the weight we intend then resume our customary manner of eating, we almost always regain the weight we lost and, perhaps, add more.

For these reasons, few nutritionists or other specialists recommend going on a diet to loose weight because they tend to be unbalanced and harsh regimes devised for quick weight loss that can be non-sustainable and can create health risks as daily fare. Instead, they recommend adoption of a healthy lifestyle that includes eating the right foods, in the right amount, and at the right time along with moving more, increasing self-regard, and focusing on living healthfully rather than attending primarily, or exclusively, to losing weight. This is what can help us experience and maintain a healthy body weight. Similarly, focusing on learning methods and techniques to manage our stuttering can leave us disappointed if we do not also communicate more, more often, and in more diverse ways and cultivate positive, unconditional self-regard.

Fearlessly Facing Fear

As we embark on a path of desired change and, then, continue along it, we learn to appreciate the need to relate more constructively to the strong emotion of fear, especially our fear of stuttering and all that means to us personally. That fear untended can lead us to resist stuttering every which way, which, ultimately, represents the core of our stuttering problem. Acknowledging and skillfully managing our fear of stuttering, rather than repressing it, or resisting it in other ways, such as letting our partners-in-life speak for us, is the key component of learning to speak and live more as we wish. What we need to learn is to acknowledge, to accept, and to skillfully relate to being afraid without being afraid of being afraid. That skill, almost of itself, leads to speaking and communicating with greater ease.

Concurrently, we need to recognize and address our seemingly innate fear of change, even change we say we desire. As human beings, we tend to prefer certainty to uncertainty, the known to the unknown, safety to risk. So, when we contemplate speaking and living as we wish, we commonly experience the polarity of wanting change and fearing it. We know instinctively the change we want can disrupt the seemingly orderly and predictable life we live but would rather not, and we are uncertain whether or not we might feel comfortable and enjoy living differently, even though we think that is what we wish. This uncertainty can be sufficient for us to choose to continue living with the pain we know rather than entering the unknown, a prospect that can be terrifying for anyone, whether or not they have a stuttering problem.

Changing how we speak will change how we live. We know that. That is why we consider changing how we speak, or not. Managing the anxiety this awareness generates can take time. So, if and when we near the starting line to follow a path we believe will help us speak more as we wish, we can freeze and back-off. We fear facing the uncertainty or the probability of what taking that path may bring. We recognize that speaking as we wish may require us to assume responsibilities in our personal relationships and at work that we do not want to undertake or feel capable of handling well. Or we may fear seeking opportunities to become more independent and responsible by speaking up as we wish may bring unpleasant challenges, such as divorce, termination of employment, and others we may not yet suspect.

While the fear of changing to speak as we desire has not been investigated so thoroughly in relation to changing from someone who has a stuttering problem to speaking and living as someone who stutters now and then as it has in relation to losing excess body weight, I know from personal experience and from working with clients that this fear needs to be skillfully addressed for those who wish to speak with greater ease and to do so more consistently. And while I share how the secular practice of mindfulness has helped me relate constructively to fear rather than to resist it, I realize others may apply different methods to do so. But I encourage all who read this book to consider the powerful, time-tested, cognitive-behavioral practice of mindfulness (e.g., Kabat-Zinn and Davidson, 2012; Salzberg, 2012) as a clear, practical way to relate directly, personally, and effectively *in real-time* to cognitive, emotional, and bodily expressions of fear that interfere with learning to speak as we wish (e.g., Silverman, 2012).

Charting a Path of Change

This sub-heading may be a bit misleading if read too quickly. We may believe what is suggested is that change is a destination, the completion of our chosen path, a mind-state, perhaps, where all will be well for us when we arrive; and we can speak as we wish from then on. But that is not what is suggested. What is stated is something quite different, as reflected in the use of the preposition "of." That word selection, almost unilaterally, expresses the intended message, namely that the path that will help us speak as we wish is *a path of on-going change,* a course that requires us to observe moment-by-moment what we are thinking, what we are telling ourselves in our heads, what sensations we are feeling in our body, what emotions we are experiencing, and what we are doing and then to rectify them so that we act moment-by-moment in ways to support our best interest. We do not wait to complete our journey before we change to be as we wish. Our journey is one of on-going change ever more approximating that which is our ideal.

Eventually, we realize no one is going to change us but us. Not because we are incorrigible but because that is just the way it is for everyone, whether or not they have a stuttering problem. No therapist, no psychologist, no psychiatrist, no counselor, no clergy, no parent, no friend, no spouse, no one at all can change us but us. We are the only one who cares enough, who knows us well enough, and who has the power enough to change the way we see the world, each other, and ourselves and, ultimately, the way we live in this world.

We recognize that to experience the change we desire requires going through a process, one that we may not be able to fully identify or appreciate at the onset or, even, later when we believe we have completed it, but a process, nonetheless, that requires us to take the reins to be our own champion. Unfortunately, for those of us who like quick results, we rarely jump directly from "A" to "Z." To experience the durable change we desire we move step-wise from "A" to "B," then from "B" to "C," then "C" to "D," and so forth, rather than leap-frogging from where we are directly to exactly where we want to be. Consequently, we develop a plan to realize what we desire to experience and how we wish to go about doing so. But our trajectory and our path is not always straight or obvious. So, we cultivate being flexible and open to what our natural curiosity brings into our awareness that may help us accumulate experience and tools we have not previously foreseen that can contribute to our journey.

Being patient helps. We can not know how long it will take before we reach a helpful insight or consistently apply a new skill to our over-arching task of speaking more as we wish, so we do not set time-limits for ourselves. But, we do not continue to do what we are doing indefinitely if we do not see signs that by doing so we are being more as we wish. We reassess periodically what we are doing and how we are doing what we are doing to assure ourselves that our practice is what we intend. Then we make whatever changes appear warranted, which can be seemingly slight, such as making an additional phone call each week for practice, or radical, such as choosing to work alone, choosing to work with a professional, or collaborating with a different member of the same profession. In this way, we keep on doing what *we* believe best serves our quest. And we do so for as long as it takes for us to feel satisfied with the way we speak and communicate to live with greater ease and happiness.

While changing is an individual task, it is not always a solitary one, if we open to the knowledge and experience of those who have or are making their own journey to be and to communicate more as they wish and to the knowledge and experience of professionals who have helped others do so. But the journey is always our own.

Others can inform us, but they can neither inspire us nor faultlessly guide us. Only we can inspire ourselves to change to be as we wish as we recognize our right to be happy and our capacity to be so. Once we commit to changing, we discover that the guidance that can lead us to speak and communicate more as we wish comes primarily from within, and it becomes more exact as we become increasingly aware of what it is we think and what it is we do when we fail to speak and live as we wish and what we think and do when we speak and live more as we wish. Simply put: Following steps others have taken or suggest we take may not always lead to the change we wish for ourselves. And, so, we ultimately choose to trust our own inner guidance to identify and follow the path most appropriate and useful for us personally at a particular point in time.

Using Helpful Assessment Metrics

As we commit to living newly chosen or freshly refined beliefs by incorporating practices into our daily life we believe will help us speak with greater ease, we want assurance doing so is serving us as we hoped to justify continuing our effort. So, our inclination can be to monitor our stuttering and our relationship to stuttering with renewed interest and intensity as soon as we embark on our chosen program of change. We look for evidence, as we typically have, we are managing our stuttering well. We gauge whether we are stuttering more or less often and with more or less intensity. And we judge whether we are speaking more freely or continuing to resist speaking when we think we may stutter.

But applying these and other familiar and similar metrics to inform us about the effectiveness of our newly adopted program may obscure the fundamental changes we are making to speak more as we wish, and basing our judgment about our plan's usefulness on these measurements may disrupt what may be our useful work to learn to speak with greater ease. Given the transitory nature of stuttering, we know that we may stutter less or not at all, more and with greater intensity, and speak freely saying exactly what we wish where, when, and to whom we wish to say it on a given day or days or clam-up whether or not we are conscientiously applying new beliefs and behaviors to address our stuttering problem. So, basing a conclusion about how well we are doing learning to speak more as we wish on such aspects of our stuttering may lead us to hastily and incorrectly conclude our effort is worthwhile, or that it is not.

We may, for instance, jubilantly decide: "I've got it! I can speak as I wish" after one or more days of speaking as we wish and prematurely discontinue our newly adopted practice of attending to our thoughts, sensations, emotions, and behaviors as we speak before we have established strong and resilient beliefs and methods to serve us well during challenging times when older and stronger unwanted thoughts and actions can prevail. And even though we may decide to continue to provide a safety net to assure we will speak and live as satisfactorily as we currently are, we may practice lackadaisically, wishfully and erroneously believing we already have achieved our aim. But with neither the firm intent nor the unyielding attention required to cultivate the durable skills required to speak more as we wish more consistently that arise from consistent, focused practice, we will not find the long-term satisfaction we seek.

Or, if we notice we continue to stutter and to do so as often or more often and as strenuously or more strenuously than usual and that we continue to refrain from saying what we want and need to say as much or more than usual for several consecutive days after we begin our new program, we may rashly and inappropriately conclude there and then we are not benefitting. We may spin that judgment a bit and decide we may be incapable of speaking with greater ease or that the strategy we have chosen will not help us, then summarily quit. And we may advise others that the strategy we had followed ". . . just doesn't work." Or, if we remain somewhat uncertain about how well the program may be serving us, we may make what we consider a prudent decision to keep on but do so in only in a token manner to spare ourselves the full measure of disappointment and resentment we might feel if we discover we had invested time and energy in a practice we had hoped would help us speak more as we wished but did not. And that cautious, ego-protective decision to practice perfunctorily can derail the opportunity we have to speak with greater ease in both the short-run and in the long-run by encouraging us to harden to the possibility that we can change to speak more as we wish.

Naturally, we want to know whether what we are doing is helping us become more as we wish as we work to change. We want assurance we are using our precious supply of time and energy effectively. And we want to hold reasonable expectations for ourselves rather than foster untenable fantasies impossible for us to realize that can depress, discourage, and delay us from ever again working to speak more as we wish. To know how we are doing without jeopardizing our wish to change, *we benefit from attending to what we think and how we act in the moment rather than on what we have realized or hope to realize.* Monitoring the congruence between our intent and our thoughts and behavior moment-by-moment provides the sound, helpful feedback we seek and need. Calm, nonjudgmental monitoring of our self-talk and how we speak or prepare to speak helps us change. Hoping does not. And neither does worrying. Wishing for a particular result distracts us from doing what we can be doing to develop the skills and attitudes we wish to use while piling on unhelpful and unnecessary stress. So does worrying. When we place our focus on what we are doing to speak and communicate more skillfully with others, such as listening attentively and observing skillfully those around us as well as our own thoughts and behavior, rather than on worrying whether we may or may not stutter, how we will manage our stuttering if we do, and how our stuttering may affect others' impression of us, we speak and communicate with greater ease and satisfaction and do so ever more consistently.

But even those skillful actions can lead us to prematurely jettison our practice and to discouragement if we do not change to be as we wish as quickly as we wish. So, we need to cultivate patience as well as consistency of practice, since changing lifestyle beliefs and behaviors, for example, limiting the amount of salt we consume to lower our blood pressure, increasing our physical activity, and changing the way we speak and communicate, may not produce observable effects for three or more weeks after we incorporate them into our daily life (e.g., Silverman, 2012a; Weil, 1995).

We realize new beliefs and behaviors become increasingly reliable with systematic, focused practice of them. But, even as we speak with greater ease more consistently, we occasionally may stutter and think about stuttering as we have previously for reasons we may never know or need to know. What we need to know and put to use is that new beliefs and emerging behaviors are neither as strong nor as durable as older, competing ones as we are establishing them. So, when we relapse into customary, unhelpful patterns of beliefs and behavior, we benefit from re-committing to the practice we have chosen to cultivate the beliefs and behaviors we prefer to live. To help us carry on, *we choose a metric of our attention and of our effort rather than the results of our effort. We monitor whether or not we are attending to and carrying-out specific helpful activities, rather than whether or not, how much, how long, and how strongly we stutter, worry about stuttering, or accommodate our life to avoiding stuttering.* And we stay the course. As we do, we come to speak and communicate more as we wish.

Altogether these themes reflect a central, over-riding orientation, that of assuming personal responsibility. To the extent we do so, we increasingly and consistently speak and live as we wish. There is no alternative to living a life of ease and satisfaction. This is what I have learned as someone who has come to live as I wish and as a therapist who has witnessed others learn to speak and live as they wish. The job of becoming our most complete and desired self is ours alone.

RESOURCES

There are many individuals who, through personal instruction or public sharing of their knowledge and experience of what can be required and what is involved changing to be more as we wish, can help us become more honestly and constructively self-aware, curious, courageous, determined, and resolute about facing personal fears; and cautiously adventuresome about finding a way or ways to meet our individual style and need for change. I have found articles, books, video tapes, CD's, DVD's , and on-line instruction on mindfulness by

Sylvia Boorstein, Pema Chödrön, Thich Nhat Hanh, Dzigar Kongtrül, Jack Kornfield, Sakyong Mipham, Sharon Salzberg, and H. H. The Dalai Lama seminal in those respects.

Other writings I have found useful for scaling my life into one more personally satisfying are those by rabbi and integral contributor to the Jewish renewal movement, Zalman Schacter-Shalomi on *kavanah*, or intention; American born Lama Surya Das on self-awareness; meditation master Chöygam Trungpa Rinpoche on establishing practical and meaningful frameworks for self-assessment; medical intuitive and student of human consciousness Caroline Myss on cherishing and enhancing our personal well-being; and psychiatrist Eric Berne on the application of transactional analysis theory for communicating more transparently and constructively with ourselves and others. Individually and collectively, these teachers highlight the power of individual belief for good or ill and help us live ever more fully, joyfully, and peacefully *as we change*. You will find among the bibliographic listings in the Reference Section references to their accessible teachings.

To speak with greater ease, physical and mental, and to do so more consistently we benefit from adopting a lifestyle centered around increasing self-awareness and self-regard that encourages greater openness. Each of us determined to do so will find a way or ways suitable for us to look beneath the surface of our behavior with courage and honesty to recognize how worthy and capable we are. For me that is the practice of mindfulness in several complementary forms (Silverman, 2012a). And that is what helped me learn to speak with greater ease, confidence, and satisfaction more consistently. As always, I trust that you will find what you need to find and follow your path and to do so safely as you persevere.

It is well-known that the process of change is a process of self-discovery and self-rectification that can present the most significant personal challenges that when faced with honesty and courage can lead to developing useful insights and skills to live ever more wisely and well. My hope is that this volume may offer some of the direction and some of the support useful to you as you follow a path to speak, to communicate, and to live with greater ease and satisfaction.

1

JASON'S SECRET: WHAT IT FEELS LIKE TO STUTTER

INTRODUCTION

I began writing *Jason's Secret* (Silverman, 2001) in 1980 although I did not know that then. In 1980, I was frustrated, very frustrated. Speech pathologists were publishing papers identifying stuttering as a laryngeal problem and nothing more. At least one well-publicized treatment program was spawned from this notion. Those of us who worked with stuttering, our own and other peoples', and studied the problem knew that viewing stuttering as a disorder of a body part was an unhealthy oversimplification. We knew that feelings associated with stuttering, anger, fear, embarrassment, and the like, leading to alienation and an intensification of these very feelings contributed mightily to the onset of the problem and its continuance. But, at that moment in history, the most vocal of our colleagues insisted that stuttering was a *laryngospasm*. Very neat. Very operant. Stop the spasms, and the problem goes away. *Not so* for many.

I decided to counter those voices. I would author a textbook addressing the role feelings play in stuttering. But, despite, my previous record of never having a manuscript rejected, my proposal received only disinterest from textbook publishers. Instead of becoming discouraged, I became bolder and decided to put my ideas before the public, to write a trade book for adults, people with stuttering problems and people who did not have stuttering problems who wanted to know about them. But I had no more success finding a publisher in that genre than I did for the textbook proposal, although I did come close to signing a contract with a publisher, but their editorial board finally decided "not enough of a market" and sent me what they intended to be an encouraging rejection note. Saddened and angered because I wasn't able to publish something that really mattered, I slipped into a form of shock and undertook no more outward action toward publication of these ideas. I did not know then where else to publish. But I never stopped thinking about how I could transmit the "truth" about stuttering.

WRITING FOR CHILDREN

Driving my car a year or so later, I had an "Ah-Hah!" moment: I would write a story for children *showing* what it was like to have a stuttering problem. Readers would feel stuttering, the physical tensions, the anxiety, the embarrassment leading to alienation, the anger. *They would learn that stuttering is not just something wrong with the way someone speaks but a particular way of seeing the world and yourself in it that can lead to profound alienation from others and your own true self.*

If I hadn't been intensely motivated to share these thoughts with others, I might have given up before I began to write. The task of learning to write fiction for children was daunting. It took years. Like anything else that looks easy, writing for children can be extremely difficult to do well. Shifting genres from scientific/technical impersonal/objective writing to fiction was a major shift, like taking up residence in a foreign country and a major undertaking, like building a rocket to fly to the moon.

Joining the Society for Children's Book Writers & Illustrators, attending "hands-on" writing conferences, workshops, and seminars where I received and offered critiques, and participating in a local writers' group for authors of children's books sharpened my focus, honed my skills, and fueled my drive. And: *I KEPT WRITING.* Jane Yolen, children's book author and editor, addressing a workshop I attended emphasized, "You're not a writer unless you're writing." Dreaming about writing and studying about writing are not writing. Only writing is writing.

I wrote. I completely revised *Jason's Secret* at least 15-20 times; I lost count. I made changes in plot and style but not in intent. I was determined to *show* what it was like to stutter, how stuttering feels in the body, how you feel about yourself, the envy you have for those who speak smoothly, the longing to be like everyone else, the fear of being thought of as a *freak*. I was determined to *show* what can be required to change into a more fluent speaker, for the child and for the adults who care about the child. And I was motivated to help children with stuttering problems break out of the sense of isolation many feel by telling a story about a 10 year-old boy who had similar experiences and feelings.

PUBLISHING

I also studied children's book publishing. I learned how to write query letters and manuscripts that could move the unsolicited manuscript through the "slush pile" into an editor's out-stretched hands. I learned about the role of agents, when and how to obtain one. And I learned about contracts and how to negotiate them. As I kept writing, I watched children's book publishing go from boom to bust as bottom-line driven conglomerates that owned most of the publishing companies demanded "best sellers." Backlists were shrunk and "kill contracts," contracts negating the original contract, were offered. New voices were no longer sought as desirable. I was extremely frustrated, saddened for myself and for everyone touched by the publishing industry, and very angry. I had developed a manuscript workshop leaders told me "needed to be published." But I doubted publishing houses that then began promoting books by personalities, television judges, movie stars, and best-selling authors of adult fiction, would publish me. Not wanting to face more agonizing rejection, busy developing my business and living my life, I literally put *Jason's Secret* on a shelf where it stayed for years.

Then, about two years ago, I heard about electronic publishing, namely *ebooks* and POD products, i.e., print-on-demand books. Electronic publishing bring authors' works quickly and economically to the public (as anyone who is a fan of Steven King knows). I chose to publish *Jason's Secret* both as an *ebook* and POD product. It had been long enough in the making. It was time for the launch. In the year 2000, the message of *Jason's Secret* no longer seems as radical as it did in 1980, but it still needs to be heard, especially by children and not just children with stuttering problems. Children with feelings of alienation leading to low self-esteem and anger management issues may find in *Jason's Secret* encouragement and direction to become their own true selves. And all children may be less likely to tease and bully a child because they have a stuttering problem after reading *Jason's Secret*.

ഔ COMMENTARY ഔ

STUTTERING AND STUTTERING PROBLEMS

Listening to someone who has a stuttering problem can trigger the belief that stuttering problems consist of glitches saying this sound or that sound or this word or that word, nothing more. Some of us with stuttering problems and some of us who offer professional help to those with stuttering problems consider this conceptualization to be complete until we encounter someone who claims to have a stuttering problem but does not stutter in our presence. Such a meeting can shock and confuse us. We question how someone who does not publically stutter can have a stuttering problem until detailed explanation and, perhaps, our own investigation reveals that some people, males and females, never or rarely stutter in public yet live in fear of stuttering. They are known as people with *interiorized*, or *covert*, stuttering problems (Rentschler, 2011; Spillers, 2011; Douglass and Quarrington, 1952). These individuals demonstrate that it is possible to have a stuttering problem without publically stuttering, and that it is impossible to have a stuttering problem, no matter how we may stutter, without fearing and resisting stuttering.

By recognizing that the heart of a stuttering problem for children and for adults is fear of stuttering, not stuttering *per se,* we come to realize that releasing ourselves from stuttering problems requires releasing ourselves from our fears about stuttering. These fears can be deeply entrenched within our mind-body system by the time we are adults, since many of us, when we are three or four years old or so with limited experience and an immature cognitive system may first experience the primal fear that arises from believing we may perish if we stutter. We may, quite literally, fear stuttering may kill us. We may fear that the loss of control of our bodies that we experience as we stutter could lead to death on-the-spot, which can become our reason to struggle intensely to quickly break free from the sensation of constriction stuttering can arouse. And some of us may believe authority figures disapproving of our stuttering and of us for stuttering may reject and abandon us leaving us to die. Later we may morph this fear into a slightly gentler imagined scenario but a similarly troubling one nonetheless. We may believe and expect that stuttering will brand us as undesirable, in certain ways, such as shy, nervous, and withdrawn, which may limit our involvement and success in the workplace and crimp our social relationships leading us to die metaphorically. This early fear we may have that by stuttering we might die through strangulation or neglect is often overlooked or underplayed by adults. Yet, with its roots embedded in our subconscious, it may be as active and tenacious a contributor to our stuttering problem as an adult as any other factor and, perhaps, more so, as it was for me.

Our fear of harm from stuttering often is exacerbated by the uncertainty of when we may stutter next. The transitory nature of stuttering can drive an ongoing subterranean vigilance that keeps us on edge psychologically and physically, which can raise our stress level and stimulate a myriad of related cognitive, linguistic, and muscular-skeletal consequences that can exacerbate our stuttering and, of course, reduce our general health, and contribute to a sense of alienation, which also can reduce our physical and emotional well-being..

So, given that our fear of stuttering represents such a formative and sustaining contributor to our stuttering problem, we realize that to speak with greater ease, we need to address that fear experientially and cognitively to know, not just grasp the idea, but to recognize in our body and in our mind that we can stutter and live, both literally and figuratively. I personally have found the practice of various forms of mindfulness taught from within the Tibetan Buddhist tradition especially helpful, focusing as they do, on the primacy of learning to acknowledge and skillfully relate to what we think, feel, and sense in the moment (Silverman, 2012a). In so doing, I have learned the distinction between stuttering and stuttering *problems* derived from the fear of stuttering to accept the one and to resolve the other.

2

CONSUMER ALERT: STUTTERING AND GENDER RESEARCH

INTRODUCTION

Scientists Confuse with Conflicting Reports

What foods to safely eat is more a question than ever to many who rely on scientists' recommendations. During the past decade alone, scientists in the United States have promulgated a bevy of confusing directives. For instance, they have warned us that eggs raise cholesterol levels and endanger cardiovascular health only to later rescind that *caveat* and state eggs really do belong in a healthy diet. They have told us coffee is unhealthy, only to later state that that caffeinated beverage is not harmful if consumed in moderation. They have encouraged us to eat pasta only to caution us recently that high carbohydrate consumption can trigger adult onset diabetes. And so on. People have become so confused about what is safe to eat they are choosing foods primarily for taste, i.e., those high in fat content. Doing so has contributed to an alarming trend: Estimates suggest 50% of the population, including children, is now clinically obese.

This example says a lot about science, scientists, and consumers. While science may be an exact method, its application can be flawed. Research questions derived from scientists' incomplete knowledge of the whole, desire for recognition, and/or unwitting personal biases can lead to inadequate results, possibly harmful ones. A contemporary example is investigations into AIDS. Not long ago, researchers stated the disorder could be adequately managed by drugs. Those who had been taking the especially designed medications for several years have now demonstrated both the truth and untruth of that pronouncement: AIDS does respond to medication, but the drugs that manage the disease only do so until the virus mutates into a drug intolerant form. Then, only new drugs may be effective. Another, perhaps, unexpected effect was relaxation of the dread about the disease. Many young gay men believing AIDS was no longer a serious problem began disregarding safe sex practices. The incidence of new cases of AIDS in the United States is now increasing rapidly.

Consumers of research findings once again have been harmed by taking recommendations at face value. We need to learn there is no adequate substitute for personal responsibility. Science alone can not answer all our questions personally and collectively at the time we most want answers. To think otherwise may be to succumb to one of the greatest temptations of all time.

Research on Stuttering

Stuttering research, too, has had its share of follies. The vocal fold theory of the '70's, the stimulus - response approach to treatment in the '60's, the cerebral dominance theory of the '30's.all promised more than they ever delivered. And all, since they were championed by persuasive individuals, managed to shut-down almost all dissent of contemporaries. But most stuttering research efforts in the United States have been contaminated by one major, flawed assumption. Namely, that stuttering behavior could be studied satisfactorily essentially independent of individuals. Gender, race, social group, ethnic origin all were dismissed as meaningless variables. Group rather than single-subject research design was the preferred method. Groups consisting of quasi-people were studied, not individuals. In all fairness, this was true of many programs of inquiry into the nature of human behavior until quite recently. But, since that was true, what does that say about the findings of so much research into the nature of stuttering and of treatment efficacy? To whom can these findings be generalized?

TRUTH SEEKING

I want to know what really is regardless of how I prefer things to be.

- - - Charles Tart, Psychologist.

In the mid - 1970's, based on my own experience and that of a client, I decided to conduct a natural experiment into the effect of anxiety on stuttering. Rather than simulating anxiety as it had customarily been done by administering electric shocks to participants or by threatening to do so, I decided to compare women's fluency at two points in the menstrual cycle. By then, it was well known that, because of quite specific fluctuations in hormone levels, namely that of estrogen and progesterone, women, as a group, demonstrated increased feelings of well-being at mid-cycle and increased anxiety during the premenstrual portion of the cycle. I wasn't considering at the time that data on women were generally lacking. I, as most investigators, tacitly accepted the rationale advanced through casual analysis by investigators, almost all of whom were male, that males were the subject of choice because they were more accessible, since more males than females were university students, individuals who typically comprised the pool of subjects drawn upon for study, and they were more appropriate, since more males than females seemed to develop stuttering problems.

I realized only later, after completing the initial investigation (Silverman *et. al,* 1974) and two related ones (Silverman and Zimmer, 1975; Silverman and Zimmer, 1976) that that assumption that gender was irrelevant to the nature and treatment of stuttering problems was unsupportable. So, in the context of the times, when the scientific community began to recognize men and women may not only be hard-wired differently but may also hold different world views, I then undertook research into gender differences in stuttering demographics, stereotyping, treatment preferences, treatment experiences, and attitudes toward communication (Silverman and Zimmer, 1979, Silverman, 1980; Silverman and Van Opens, 1980; Silverman and Zimmer, 1982a; Silverman and Zimmer, 1982b; Silverman, 1986).

This program of research uncovered distinct differences between male and female stutterers in demographics, stereotyping (including the distinct likelihood at the time it was conducted that elementary school teachers were less likely to refer a girl for stuttering therapy than a boy presenting the exact same symptoms, i.e., Silverman and Van Opens, 1980), treatment preferences and experiences, and approach to interpersonal communication. Yet, insofar as I am aware, these findings, summarized in "The Female Stutterer" (Silverman, 1986), have gone largely unnoticed except in a most peculiar manner. Considerable snickering and some outrage greeted the efforts and findings when mentioned in my presence. Here is one especially vivid example:

In 1976, I attended the Annual Convention of the Wisconsin Speech and Hearing Association (as it was called then). At the luncheon, I sat at a table with my colleague and good friend, Catherine Zimmer, a founding

12

member of the Association. Catherine was seated on my right and a woman I did not know on my left. Throughout the meal, the woman made no effort to speak with me. In fact, when I attempted to speak to her, she turned away, avoiding me. I seemed to be provoking her in some way I did not understand at first. Finally, later, as the dishes were being cleared prior to the business meeting and program, she leaned across me to force eye contact with Catherine. As she captured Catherine's attention, she barked, "How could a dignified person like you do such filthy research like that?" then, just as abruptly, she returned to her pre-question pose, much like a turtle pulling itself tightly into its shell. She said nothing more to either of us after that, nor did she even look our way. Catherine, for as long as I have known her, has never been at a loss for what to say to anyone. But she immediately became silent and quite introspective following that bizarre critique. So did I. Catherine and I knew immediately the woman at the table was referring to our paper,

"Speech fluency fluctuations during the menstrual cycle," (Silverman and Zimmer, 1975) published several months earlier. To this date, our research identifying and describing gender differences in stuttering rankles some people, amuses others, and basically is viewed as an oddity, certainly not serious science.

Unfortunately, that view should not be surprising. Scientists and professionals in the West frequently take that stance with non-mainstream research programs and findings because they are people first and foremost. And, as people, these scientists and professionals often tend to prefer the expected to the unexpected, the known to the unknown, unlike those with Eastern world views, who typically welcome, even become excited, by novel happenings believing such events better reveal the essence of life.

The fact remains that people seeking help with stuttering problems are just that, people. And the information that therapists have and still tend to receive from those conducting research and writing books, i.e., primarily means, standard deviations, etc., simply doesn't address that fact very well. The Method of Science with all its assumptions about reality from a particular human perspective, including the need for objectivity of the so-called observer, linearity of experience, and the uses of inferential and descriptive qualitative statistical analyses to interpret observations simply can not, at this point in space-time, generate information completely useful to modify behaviors of multi-tasking, complexly functioning human beings. Personal, more than impersonal, knowledge is required to inaugurate, modify, stabilize, and maintain behavioral change.

THE RESCUE TRIANGLE

Simply put: In all therapy encounters, the adult who stutters must take the driver's seat when setting goals, selecting methods, and deciding the nature and length of treatment. No one else is better equipped to do that. And to abdicate that responsibility in favor of another is to provide someone with power they may be unable to manage well.

The "Rescue Triangle" first described by Eric Berne, founder of Transactional Analysis, diagrams troublesome interactions that lead to disappointments in relationships, including therapy ones, when the tendency to allow another control over our lives and the tendency we have to want control another collide. In this series of interactions, or psychological game, there are three roles to be taken by two participants: Rescuer, Victim, and Persecutor. The Rescuer believes his or her task is to manage the other's life. The Victim believes someone else, i.e., a Rescuer, needs to tell them how to live. And the Persecutor, formerly the Rescuer or the Victim, provokes feelings of shame and/or failure in the other ending the game with unpleasant feelings abounding. Here is an example:

Steve, a 29 year-old, who has enrolled in therapy almost continually since he was six and began stuttering while reading aloud in class, feels the need to continue treatment. Despite the fact he is successful in a responsible position, has a partner in life, and enjoys a cordial circle of friends, he feels he could be more successful if he no longer stuttered. He places himself in the role of Victim searching for a therapist (Rescuer) by verbally and non-verbally saying, "I need your help. Only You can help me." But Steve, in so-doing, is not honest with himself. He believes no one "out there" is able to change him from a person who stutters into someone who does not. In fact, Steve believes that since no speech therapist has cured him, none ever will. And what he really wants to do is rub that in the face of any therapist who takes his Victim bait. He does that by entering a therapy relationship with a therapist eager to be the one to change him. To prove himself correct, he resists all suggestions and recommendations the therapist makes, until the therapist, out of frustration, dismisses him or he chooses to directly say he has not benefitted from treatment and quits.

Then the game ends with the therapist angry and feeling like a failure, possibly distressed enough to avoid working with others who have stuttering problems, i.e., becoming Victim. While Steve, feeling superior at this point, at first feels good letting the therapist know just how incompetent he thinks he or she is, i.e., becoming Persecutor, but shortly feels bad when he returns to the thought he is incurable. Playing out the "Rescue Triangle" is like running around in a circle, never going anywhere new and getting increasingly angry and tired.

If a person with a stuttering problem wants to be a person without a stuttering problem, then a radical change in thinking is required. And that is to realize and believe that "The only one who is going to change me is Me!"

TAKING CHARGE

Clients as potential consumers of therapy services need to be informed not only about therapeutic resources but what they want and or need and what they're willing to do to get that. That is how to successfully use valuable knowledge and skills of speech-language pathologists: As resources and coaches. In reality, there is nothing more speech-language pathologists can do for their clients!

SUMMARY

To expect science and speech-language pathologists utilizing scientific methods primarily aligned with statistical models of probability to unilaterally or primarily facilitate favorable clinical outcomes while we as consumers adopt a passive role toward realizing greater self-mastery is to be sorely disappointed at this point in space-time. People with stuttering problems and those who care for them are the ones who know best what is desired for personal change and the ones best positioned to take primary responsibility to foster it. There is no viable alternative to taking personal responsibility to experience a favorable therapy outcome.

ಞ COMMENTARY ಞ

SELF-STUDY

Some of us believe therapists will guide us to what we need to know. And some of us believe researchers will. But eventually we discover we can and need to be our own pathfinders.

To be as we wish, many of us look to clinicians, who look to the work of researchers, to tell us what to do to speak with greater ease. But, although clinicians and researchers have studied stuttering, stuttering problems, and people with stuttering problems for almost a century in the United States alone, we are not necessarily likely to encounter a clinician willing and able to partner with us to provide the personalized direction we seek to help us change from being a person with a stuttering problem to a being person who stutters now and then. The odds are stacked us, given the relatively small number of interested and suitably prepared professionals locally and globally. Complicating and compounding the likelihood that we may locate a clinician to safely and surely guide us to speak more as we wish is the statistical database clinicians draw upon to create therapy protocols. Generated by conducting studies designed to satisfy assumptions commonly associated with quantitative research design methodologies, that pool of research findings may not optimally translate to information useful for individuals desiring to change as they wish (e.g., Creswell, 2008).

Quantitative research design methodology derives from the assumption that what needs to be known is to be found in the world outside ourselves through a crafted process of observation expected to be objective and uninfluenced by the observer and the act of observation. Qualitative research design, on the other hand, a method which has found favor among social scientists since it was proposed in the early 1900's to understand *how* and *why* individuals make decisions, recognizes an inherent connection between all beings, observers and observed alike, and the inevitability that the observer's presence and values affect the observed. Similar to certain healing practices, such as transactional analysis (e.g., Berne, 1996; Woollams and Brown, 1979), narrative medicine (e.g., Charon, 2008), and narrative speech pathology (Silverman, 2008a), qualitative research design seeks to uncover the needs and goals of the observed without imposing the observer's beliefs as to what that is or should be.

So, those of us who wish to leave our stuttering problems behind and who have come to believe a professional must show us how to do that can become quite morose and even agitated when we

17

discover we need to rely on ourselves for guidance and support. That we can forge our own path to solve our own problems initially can be a surprising and, even, unsettling conclusion for some of us whose family, culture, and society may have encouraged us to believe that others, not we, will remove our problems, or at least show us how we can do so. So, when we recognize we may not have access to experts able to care for us as we have been taught to expect, we can feel quite sad and angry for a time. We can feel betrayed, abandoned, and, possibly, bereft.

We realize we are on our own, and we feel frightened. We believe with no one knowledgeable and skilled to help us change we may live as an outsider until the very end. Then we feel even more fear. And our fear may morph into considerable anger slowly or quite quickly if we believe we have been denied our entitlement of meaningful care from professionals our culture may encourage us to believe are responsible for and to us. Anger we do not wish to reveal or, even, admit to ourselves because we were discouraged from feeling anger when we were young. Anger that, metaphorically, can rot our gut, sour our disposition, and boil our blood.

So, some of us, unaware of other options, "whistle a happy tune" whenever we feel afraid, as the song lyrics suggest. Or we may camouflage our fear of failure by expressing our angry thoughts indirectly through cynical and sarcastic remarks occasionally punctuated by a furious outburst here and there. Those tactics may work for a while as a distraction from the pain we feel. They even may embolden us as we experience a sense of power and strength that comes from recognizing the power of our mind to create our experience and that we can intimidate others. And that rush of pride and satisfaction can release the prickly energy of the fear we may not make it in this world that, otherwise, may become intense sadness. But, eventually, we realize pretense and our cynical and blustery ways may not be helping us get the satisfying relief from our stuttering problem we want. They may, instead, be causing mounting challenges in personal and work relationships that render us feeling remote, embattled, and confused rather than accepted and confident. Recognizing all that, we may, if we are fortunate, open to knowledge and experience that assures us we can find our own way to resolve our stuttering problem. As that thought lands, we instantly may feel relief and a new vitality. We feel refreshed, no longer oppressed.

We recognize that the process of changing to be as we wish is in our hands, and that that is all right. We can take information and draw encouragement from whatever source or sources inspire us and seem reasonable and congenial. We can pick and choose what we want to do and how and how long we want to do it. We are on our own but not alone. The wisdom of all is available to us. And we recognize we do not need to please anyone but ourselves.

We take charge. We no longer believe we are dependent on others to show us the way. In reality, no one but us ever knew or ever will know what we need to change; that knowledge is ours and ours alone and always will be. When we recognize we can choose whether, when, and how we will change and that we are responsible only to ourselves, we are on our way to living a fuller and happier life. We no longer feel frustrated waiting for professionals to rescue us by telling us what we need to do and by hearing that no matter what we may do to speak and live as we wish, our stuttering problems are ours for life.

We choose to move on. We change our beliefs and change our behavior to put our stuttering problems behind us. We gain in self-knowledge. And that includes the recognition that in learning to speak and live with greater ease we can rely first and foremost on ourselves to get and do what we need. We live with greater enthusiasm and hopefulness learning it is we who will find our own way.

3

MY PERSONAL EXPERIENCE WITH STUTTERING AND MEDITATION

INTRODUCTION

I am thankful to have the opportunity to share my experiences as someone who stutters who has self-treated her particular problem rather successfully. Organizing my story and then sharing it has brought me more deeply in touch with who I am and, therefore, more capable of helping others. My story, as is anyone's, is both unique and recognizable. My experiences added to others attest to the positive results firm motivation and "personal locus of control," i.e., personal responsibility, can bring. This we all know but need reminding from time to time.

MY STUTTERING PROBLEM

In October of 2003, I will be 61 years old. On that day, I will have had a stuttering problem for 58 years! But, for 22 of those years, I didn't realize I did! I first recognized I had a problem when I was 36. And, ironically, I am a speech therapist who researched, wrote about, and provided therapy and counseling to help others deal with stuttering since I was 21. This is, perhaps, the truly unique aspect of my story.

For 33 years, I was shy, terrified to speak one-to-one and in small and large groups unless I was teaching or providing therapy or counseling. In those settings, I prepared carefully and felt emboldened, perhaps, a bit self-righteous. My only concern was to share appropriate knowledge and experience. In other settings, I felt totally inept and terrified to talk. My years of experience speaking only when I had to, and, then, mostly in classrooms left me without speech skills needed for effective discussion, argumentation, and every day conversation. By 27, having the responsibilities of developing a career, maintaining a marriage, and parenting my daughter, I was unwilling to take time to learn skills I lacked. I resigned myself to remaining in the tight little circle in which I felt comfortable and avoided other arenas. And I was afraid to admit I wasn't perfect and needed help of such a basic sort. But I had no idea underneath it all was an unresolved stuttering problem!

In my 36th year, my world changed radically. I was awarded academic tenure. No longer concentrating on achieving tenure, I suddenly had a clearer vision of my whole life: Who I was. Where I was. What I needed to do to express myself. And, importantly, I recognized I had the time and resources to develop my individuality. My over-whelming desire was to paint, a core impulse repressed until then. I soon became a Sunday painter and have not been the same since. I began to see more deeply, as is necessary to draw and paint convincingly. I began developing more synergistic impressions of life than the behaviorist outlook that had been my exclusive window on the world since beginning graduate studies allowed. In short, I was discovering my right-brain and accessing it more and more. Much later, in fact in my 60th year, I discovered my right hemisphere probably is dominant, when I serendipitously noticed I

easily signed American Sign Language with my left hand and struggled signing with my right! Previously I thought I was ambidextrous,
right hand dominant.

I began to have opinions about life and a desire to talk about
them. And, in a short while, I suddenly began stuttering severely!
Part-word repetitions of 5 or more units on the first or first several
words launched utterances that fizzled out from my bewilderment,
embarrassment, and physical discomfort with my inexplicable, loud,
conspicuous stuttering. I would experience this for days at a time
and then revert to limited speech to stop stuttering. I was frightened.

I continue to stutter as I did then, particularly when I am unable
to verbalize thought forms exciting to me as quickly as I would like.
But I have learned to make bodily adjustments in breathing, pho-
nating, and articulating, and to modify my self-perception so that
these episodes are mildly irritating and even instructive rather than
catastrophic.

During a chance encounter with an aunt and uncle I had not
seen for 12 years, I learned, that although I had spoken early and
well, I had had "a bad" stuttering problem when I was three, just
months before my mother died. They were no more specific than
that. Although, I wasn't able to consciously recall the sensation of
stuttering, I was able to remember some feelings and thoughts
immediately following my mother's shocking death at 36. Intense
psychic body aches from that abrupt, wrenching separation.
Feeling alone and terrified. Then I recalled a key thought: I would
have to take care of myself. When my mother died, I had yet to
learn to ask for what I wanted. She anticipated my every need. That
seems strangely over-protective for an elementary school teacher.
Perhaps, she was trying to shield me from the discomfort and anxiety of stuttering I was showing at the time. Taking care of myself
meant I would have to ask for what I wanted. I panicked. I didn't
know how. I entered a state of shock, which I have only recently
exited.

As I relived thoughts and feelings immediately following my mother's death, I remembered her death. Late, her first night home after giving birth to my sister, she began vomiting. The sounds terrified me. I wanted them to stop. More than that; I wanted her to be OK. I ran into my parents' bedroom, and shouted at my mother, "Shut up! Shut up!" I still can remember the look on her face when she realized how frightened I was and knowing she was incapable of comforting me. She died that night in bed. She had had a stroke. Later on, thinking as a child thinks, I believed my words killed her.

At 38, I initiated divorce proceedings from my husband and colleague of 13 years. Some of you know him. He has had a severe stuttering problem for more than 50 years. Yet, he is quite at ease talking with others and even was a college debate champion. Ironically, I had depended on him to speak for me at work and in the world at large, which he was more than happy to do, to my detriment in many ways. For the first time, I was on my own, relating to colleagues, service personnel, my daughter's teachers, and so forth. I was terrified but didn't shirk what I thought were my responsibilities. I did not anticipate stuttering, nor attend to it when it materialized. I was intent solely on meeting my responsibilities. Several years after our divorce, I left *academia*, the kindest and most welcome home I had known, to re-experience the satisfaction of being a full-time therapist.

Two years before, while studying to be a transactional analysis therapist, I recognized my life-long speech anxiety stemmed, in part, from believing I had nothing of value to say. My immediate family heaped verbal abuse on me daily to which I was forbidden to respond without risk of severe physical abuse. When I answered questions about friends or activities or offered information or opinions, what I said was ridiculed. By first grade, I was selectively mute. I rarely spoke at home or in class. I was a good student and caused no trouble. By high school, other students called me "The Quiet One."

No one, including me, referred to me as a stutterer. In fact, I had never heard the word or known of it until I was 13. Nevertheless, my subconscious memory of early childhood stuttering was contributing to personal choices and shaping my self-concept. When I encountered people labeled stutterers, including my ex-husband, I wanted to provide relief for them. But I did not make the connection between their difficulty speaking and a probable root cause of my own speech anxiety.

No one referred me for speech therapy although I lived in a large metropolitan area. Ironically, when I entered college, I was excited to major in speech correction, as speech therapy was then called. I looked forward to sparing children difficulty communicating with others, without being consciously aware that, by doing so, I might be helping myself.

By graduation, I had discovered the joy of writing, through which I could express my thoughts and feelings without anxiety. Writing continues to be my preferred mode of interpersonal communication. But, having built a successful business during the last seven and one-half years, I have learned effective business communication skills and have lost all limiting apprehensions about negotiations and discussions.

MEDITATION PRACTICES AND BENEFITS

Studying and applying Transactional Analysis first convinced me I could learn to communicate successfully, although learning to ask for what I wanted was so difficult at first that I almost quit half-way into my first class. Blushing, sweating, looking at the floor but not seeing it, hearing my heart thumping while stating what I wanted from training group members was excruciating. I did not stutter, but I was extremely hesitant. Unlike other communication situations, this one required me to associate thoughts and feelings with my behavior and work them out. My usual complaining and

25

self-pity were unacceptable. Despite the intense anxiety this process provoked, I knew this training was right for me. I continued, practiced, learned, changed, and changed some more. I learned rules for communicating clearly and concisely. It helped that our trainer had been born in Australia and was educated in England and valued precise speech! And she tolerated no excuses and did not credit anyone with trying, only with changing. A very good environment for me!

We were a diverse group consisting of nurses, social workers, clergy, classroom teachers, counselors, and therapists. Through my contact with individual members, I learned of meditation. Initially, I learned the value of visualization. I was convinced as I witnessed thoughts relax my body and induce rhythmic, deep breathing that the mind affects the body. At this point, I was not attending to my stuttering in a direct manner. My attention was more encompassing. I was addressing my need to become a competent communicator and to use my mind to positively influence my body. Experience with visualization led me to the practice of meditation. Earlier, I had practiced transcendental meditation, a meditation technique imported from India popular in the early 1970's and considered somewhat exotic. I did not find sufficient benefit for the time required and practiced only sporadically.

Not until the mid-1980's when I immersed myself in the study of spirituality and religion and established a practice of daily prayer, did I re-visit meditation as a disciplined personal practice. A friend offered me a primer on Buddhism. I read the slim volume, impressed by the assertion that life is difficult but that we can free ourselves from suffering by appropriate action. But I was more than a little frightened by a practice arising from an Eastern culture. I somehow over-looked the Eastern genesis of Judaism and Christianity and that I had practiced Transcendental Mediation earlier! Because I desired to not suffer and to be happy, I soon began daily study and practice of Theravadan and Tibetan Buddhist meditation techniques and yoga. I continue to do so.

Not then, nor since, have I directly addressed my stuttering. But it is no longer a problem. Why? Daily study and meditation practices help me calm and strengthen my mind and modify my outlook and behavior. I have accumulated the following benefits, all of which are known to reduce the frequency and severity of stuttering:

1. Reduced personal and existential anxiety

2. Increased body awareness

3. Heightened mental clarity

4. Acceptance of personal responsibility

5. Increased personal acceptance

I have learned that I can present myself competently through speech and other ways and that, should I stutter, I am no more or less of a person than when I do not. I do not like the feel of stutter-ing. I am frightened by losing control of my body. But I am learning to appreciate the opportunity stuttering provides to release my need for complete control. I value sensitive listening and caring, compas-sionate, truthful speech. I place a premium on my personal percep-tions. I take full responsibility for solving my problems. I believe I am no better nor no worse than anyone else.

I still talk little but no longer because I'm afraid. I prefer to think and do rather than talk. I embrace the biblical admonition to avoid idle speech and the Buddhist practice of "Right Speech."

CONCLUSION

What I have learned is that "locus of control" is key. When we accept we can either consciously control ourselves or be con-trolled by subconscious influences, we can constructively live our lives, despite any difficult childhood experiences we may have had.

A March, 2003, article by Pema Chödrön (2003a), a Buddhist nun, published in *Shambhala Sun*, provides insight and direction into one method of overcoming urges, i.e., *shenpa*, especially habitual ones. She likens *shenpa* to a fish hook and identifies tensing as the first sign we are hooked. Chödrön describes the stages involved in working with *shenpa* as four R's: "... recognizing the *shenpa*, refraining from 'scratching,' relaxing into the underlying urge to scratch, and then resolving to continue to interrupt our habitual patterns like this for the rest of our lives."

∞ COMMENTARY ∞

PERSONAL STORY

Whether or not we have a stuttering problem, other people's lives intrigue us. What our friends, co-workers, and family members do interest us, as do the activities of neighbors, acquaintances, and strangers. We want to know how they and others, especially those featured in the media, live. We recognize their lives mirror our own and our hopes and expectations for our own. Learning about how they live their lives ultimately teaches us more about how to live our own. We see more clearly what we do, what we do not do, what we want to do, and what we do not want to do. From their example, we identify personal attributes as well as previously unrecognized talents we want to cultivate and qualities we despise and do not want to develop or want to squelch. And we can deepen our own innermost inclination to live more meaningfully by carefully considering others' courageous and indefatigable responses to personal, family, and community challenges. But our fascination with others' lives can have a problematic aspect. Observing others' lives more closely than our own, we divert ourselves from constructively facing what we would rather avoid or deny, the fearful uncertainty, the annoying ordinariness, and the painful element of loss we experience in our lives. This tendency to avoid the unpleasantness of our lives delays or blunts our opportunity for developing tools to skillfully address what we consider unpleasant.

Those of us with stuttering problems often like to know about others who have or have had stuttering problems. We join *list-serv's*, read blogs, attend online conferences, and buy books to develop a more expansive understanding of how people effectively manage their stuttering problems, or not. Knowing others, too, have and have had stuttering problems, yet live meaningful lives inspires us. We begin to believe, or strengthen our belief, that we, too, can live well. Knowing that some have found ways to overcome their stuttering problems to live as people who may stutter now and then encourages us. Their stories affirm our conviction that we, too, can find a way or ways to resolve our problem. We even may consider taking all or some of the steps they did to learn what they have to speak more as we wish.

Or we may take a darker road. Comparing how they have come to speak with greater ease with our continuing effort to speak with-out struggle, we may become bitter, resentful that some are experiencing what we want but still have not achieved and, perhaps, never will. Setting such obstructive beliefs into motion may weaken our commitment to do what we can to speak as we wish. We may stop searching for the tools that may help, stop practicing to develop or hone the tools we need for the work we need and want to do, and, most damaging, stop feeling excited about taking charge of our lives. This is how personal comparisons become odious, when we use them to reinforce a disharmonious sense of competition, a belief that others have "won" and we have "lost." But we do not need to believe others' success diminishes us. The reality is that others' success can strengthen us. By looking deeply into the causes and conditions for their delight and re-examining our own motivations, abilities, and challenges, we can discover how we, too, may experience what we wish. That may be by doing what they have done, some of what they have done, or none of what they have done, but following a seemingly different path that we find congenial. Their success can remind us there is enough opportunity for us all to live more as we wish. Believing that, we fare better. We can relax into our lives to constructively develop and apply strategies to help us speak and live with greater ease and satisfaction.

Knowing that others' stories have benefited us, we may decide to share our experience learning to speak with greater ease as a story we, too, can share, although, for those close to us, the way we live day-to-day already reveals much of what we have learned. But, should we decide to share our experience more widely through writing or telling of it, we may be surprised to realize how we ourselves benefit. Fashioning our experiences, feelings, and insights into a story to invite others to re-consider what is true, what is possible, and what is necessary to live with ease of mind, body, and heart can also help us see ourselves and lives more clearly to clear the way for further growth.

We start by dispassionately reviewing our life with the intent of understanding what has been and what remains meaningful to us (e.g., Hellman, 1973). Like any other art form, assembling a montage of remembrance into physical form, oral, written, and/or video, can open our eyes. Done with honesty, perspective, and proportion, we discover what we presently know to be true about ourselves and others, which may differ from the beliefs we have been living. We recognize we may have been acting as a young child in an adult body. Like Josh, the 13 year-old lead character of the movie *Big* (1998), who magically turns into a 30 year-old overnight but maintains the sensibilities of his 12 year-old self, we may have grown physically while continuing to live the way our young self believed was essential to be safe to survive. We see we have been living minute-by-minute according to the beliefs we formed about ourselves, others, and the world when we were preschoolers, children, and teens. These beliefs developed by an immature cognitive system fueled by limited knowledge and experience in this world often continue to shape our thoughts, direct our actions, and prompt and color our emotions in the most fundamental and subtle ways. They establish our outlook and choreograph our lives (e.g., Berne, 1996; Steiner, 1994). And they comprise the core of our stuttering problem until we change or replace them

Consider how some of us with stuttering problems refer to those with whom we speak, hope to speak, or intend to speak. We call them *our listeners*. Doing so, we create a *scenario* in which we imbue those individuals with the characteristic of judge or critic whose job it is to attend primarily, if not exclusively, to us and the adequacy of our actions and behavior according to their standards, rather than to our feelings and the content of our message or inquiry. In this parallel inter-personal arrangement we devise, we assume the role of performer dependent on their good will and vulnerable to their rejection. And, among the primary criteria we believe they apply to judge us are whether or not we stutter and, perhaps, how we stutter. Such an unhealthy perception of communication formed when we were young and vulnerable when left unchallenged can reside within our subconscious mind and continue to color, if not direct, how we approach speaking and communicating. Discovering we continue to live such an untruth can be startling. As adults, we have come to appreciate intellectually that every-day speaking is a means of communicating not performing *per se* and that those with whom we speak are not stand-in's for the adults of our childhood who, we may have believed, cared more about whether or not we stuttered than what we had to say. But that may not be how we live moment-by-moment.

We know from experience we will survive whether we stutter or not. Setting aside our embarrassment at discovering that we as adults have been living a code of conduct formulated by our child self, which most of us do until we awake whether or not we have a stuttering problem (e.g., Berne, 1996; Jung, 1986: von Franz, 1964), we work at internalizing this fresh awareness of reality. That includes forgiving ourselves for creating roadblocks for ourselves and, perhaps, for others by living as we have and, perhaps, those who deliberately, or otherwise, distracted us from speaking as we wished by expecting us to conform to their ideals.

Our personal story can transport us to a satisfying present and, perhaps, an even more satisfying future. That is possible when we realize it does not end until we do or until we lay it aside, as do some, for example Buddhists, to experience *nirvana*. We can view the story we have assembled about our life as a narrative vehicle subject to up-dating as we widen our experience and perspective. We recognize this provisional assemblage of experience and belief as a concept more or less helpful to us and, perhaps, to others as a tool for discovering meaning and drawing direction. In this way, we recognize our story, as any personal story, can serve as a touch-stone for our evolving path to become ever more fully who and what we are, which includes speaking and living with ever increasing ease, or not.

4

USING STORY TO HELP HEAL

⌘

It seems plain and self-evident; yet it needs to be said: The isolated knowledge obtained by a group of specialists in a narrow field has in itself no value whatsoever, but only in its synthesis with all the rest of knowledge and only inasmuch as it really contributes in this synthesis toward answering the demand, Who are we?

- - - C. Erwin Schrodinger, 1933 Nobel Prize Laureate in Physics

⌘

A tourist noticed three men working on an urban lot where a synagogue was being erected. Approaching one, she asked, 'What are you doing?' 'I am a stone mason, the man answered. I cut stone. That is what I do.' Turning to the second, she asked, 'What are you doing?' 'I am a brick layer,' the worker replied. 'I lay bricks. That is what I do.' Addressing the remaining worker, sweeping the area with a broom, she asked, 'What are you doing?' 'I am building a beautiful temple for God and the people,' he answered smiling.

- - - My Re-telling of an Hasidic Teaching Tale

INTRODUCTION

Think what our world would be like without story. No myths, tales, fables, folklore, dreams, anecdotes, history or, even, gossip to shape us. How different our family, culture, and society would be. How different we would be. It is almost unimaginable, like contemplating the sound of a song that has no melody. Story comprises the fabric of our lives. Knowing that, we can use story to help ourselves change.

STORY

Story helps fashion who we are and who we think we are, what we are and what we may expect to become. Stories told to form our perception of ourselves, the world around us, and our place in that world exist in earliest recorded history. They abound in the Hebrew Scriptures, referred to by some as *The Old Testament.* These stories of epic creation and destruction, relationship, partnership, civility, obedience, and passion inform and sharpen our perceptions leading to shared values and behavior, as do their counterparts in many other traditions (Campbell, 1988; Fraser, 1923). They function as a staple of rabbinic teaching (e.g., Polsky and Wozner, 1989) including that of Jesus The Christ who taught primarily through parable. By activating multiple sensory channels while recounting common experience, stories serve as teaching tools that indelibly reach not only the mind but the heart. Story tellers, revered throughout history and across cultures as depositories of prized human experience, use these riches to teach and heal (Estés, 1993). Clarissa Pinkola Estés, Jungian analyst and story teller in the *Latina* tradition, elaborates (1993, pp 4-5):

. . . many of the most powerful medicines, that is stories, come about as a result of one person's or a group's terrible and compelling suffering. For the truth is that much of story comes from travail, theirs, ours, mine, yours, someone's we know, someone's we do not know far away in time and place. And, yet, paradoxically, these very stories that rise from deep suffering can provide the most potent remedies for past, present, and even future ills.

So, too, fictional stories can heal. Written to expose layers of the human soul and the world political by keen observers of humanity, such as Aesop, Leo Tolstoy, Henrik Ibsen, Franz Kafka, Toni Morrison, Gabriel García Márquez, C. S. Lewis, Lois Lowry, J.K. Rowling, and Maurice Sendak, they guide us to our place and contribution in the world.

Children with stuttering problems experience stories as guides to self awareness and sources of inspiration as all children do as they open to their messages. I still remember sitting on my grandfather's lap when I was four asking him to repeat a particular folk tale that only he told me. I did not quite understand the main character, the circumstances of his life, or the essential meaning of the tale, but the story riveted me. Thinking the way a child does, I thought hearing it again would make its meaning clear to me, so I asked my grandfather to repeat it. He did over and over until I no longer asked to hear it, not because I understood it but because I didn't and did not believe I could. Many years later facing a critical personal challenge as a middle-aged person, I spontaneously recalled that story and discovered the valuable meaning it held for me then.

Biographies saved my life. When I was eight, I discovered a series of stories in our school library about famous people when they were children. As I digested one after another, I came to believe that, like all the main characters, I, too, could survive and even succeed, if, like them, I was good, lived what I believed no matter what, and worked hard and well as long as necessary.

Stories about others are not the only ones to influence our thinking and behavior. By the time we are three, we are scripting, casting, and acting out our own life stories. Shakespeare penned in *As You Like It*: "All the world is a stage, and all the people are the actors." Loretta LaRoche (1995), stress management consultant and humor therapist, admonishes us to sharpen our self-perception by acknowledging the scripted nature of our lives. She asks quite seriously: "Do you get it yet? You are the director of your own movie."

Many prominent therapists believe living a scripted life in unawareness leads to cumulative personal dissatisfaction. For example, psychiatrist and founder of Transactional Analysis, Eric Berne (1977), helped people heal themselves by showing how to identify limiting, essentially subconscious, scripted behaviors and replace them with purposeful, skilled actions. Psychologist Daniel Goleman (1985), author of *Emotional Intelligence* (Goleman, 1995), advises us to examine the stories we tell about ourselves and the world to flush out the lies that foster delusion and court unhappiness. The discipline of journaling, for example the private Intensive Journal Program developed by Ira Progoff and the public sharing of thought and experience known as *blogging*, identifies certainties that limit our perception of reality, especially our own potential.

Spiritual teachers in Buddhist, Native American, and Judaic traditions also believe in the necessity of living a mindful existence to heal. The teachings of the 14th Dalai Lama, e.g., (2001) and zen master Thich Nhat Hanh (2000) detail methods for increasing personal awareness. Caroline Myss (1997), medical intuitive, reports an anecdote identifying one Native American approach to healing. According to Dr. Myss, a Navajo World War II veteran heeded the recommendations of his tribal council to "...reclaim his spirit..." through the recollection and then release of his experience as a POW in Nazi Germany. As a result of his modified perception and relationship to that aspect of his past, he regained the use of his wounded and wasted legs. *Kabbalists*, i.e., Jewish mystics, believe our individual stories highlight teachings of the *Torah* (Gafni, 2004). They call on us to claim and share our stories as the gifts each of us brings into this world.

Citizens of the United States have been writing personal and family stories at an unprecedented volume during the past decade or so, ostensibly to give as gifts of love to dear ones. Telling personal stories helps complete our life's journey, for many of us sense a life unshared is a life not fully lived.

Using Story as an Adjunct to Treatment

Bibliotherapy and *narrative speech pathology* can help heal. Because this conference focuses on the needs of children and adolescents, I will comment on the application of each to their needs and imagine you will be able to see possibilities they hold for adults.

BIBLIOTHERAPY

Bibliotherapy, first used in the United States with hospitalized World War I veterans, was applied to children for the first time in 1946, but only indirectly. Experts provided parents guides to help them select books to underscore desired societal values (Agnes, 1946). As children's literature changed from pedantic moralizing to presenting the world through a child's eyes and from idealizing painless circumstances to portraying challenging life situations, such as death, Alzheimer's Disease, AIDS, disabilities, divorce, and gay parents, *bibliotherapy* with children and adolescents shifted to child-centered experiential learning with the revised goal of helping children overcome their problems.

Not unexpectedly, given the relatively low incidence of stuttering and presumed low readership demand, few published stories depict a child wrestling with the various dimensions of a real-life stuttering problem. That is precisely why I wrote *Jason's Secret* (Silverman, 2001), a middle reader novel where a 10 year-old deals with his feelings about stuttering, communicating, and speech therapy, without a saccharine ending. Two other books also have *bibliotherapeutic* application: *Ben Has Something to Say* (Lears, 2000), a picture story book depicting a boy momentarily overcoming his fear of stuttering through concern for a dog, and *Sometimes I Just Stutter* (de Geus, 1999) containing several anecdotes from children and teens who stutter and one fairy tale about stuttering. These three are not the only books showcasing children with stuttering problems, but, in my opinion, they are best suited to *bibliotherapy*.

What makes *bibliotherapy* effective is:

1. Reading about other children of approximately the same chronological age who have faced problems they face helps readers better manage feelings of isolation and

2. Considering a character's thoughts, feelings, and emotions helps:

   o Identify and express feelings
   o Develop awareness that problems can be solved, including their own
   o Enhance problem-solving skills
   o Amplify social skills

With the current interest in reality programming on television, children and teens may find comparing their lives to that of book characters more compelling than ever.

Bibliotherapy can be conducted with an individual or in a group. While many respond well, some do not. Those unable to: 1) See themselves and their lives reflected through book characters, 2) Face their problems, and/or 3) Readily transfer new insights into daily life require other interventions to help them develop a realistic, helpful perception of the process of change.

NARRATIVE SPEECH PATHOLOGY

In *narrative speech pathology*, a term I coined after learning of *narrative medicine*, the fast-growing medical practice where story trumps questionnaire in diagnosis and treatment (Thernstrom, 2004), the process is consumer-centered. The narrative specialist, possessing "... competence to recognize, absorb, interpret and be moved by the stories of illness..." (Thernstrom, 2004, p. 44) encourages clients to share their histories uninterrupted while practicing analytical listening to both the content and form of the narrative, e.g., its temporal course, images, associated subplots, silences, where the tellers first begin telling of themselves, and how they sequence symptoms with their other life events.

Practitioners write their stories of patient care using a process called *Parallel Charts*. They analyze the structural elements of their writing using *narratology*, a formalist literary theory applied to story, which focuses on structure, i.e., elements of contingency, intersubjectivity (relationship of writer to subject and reader), genre, and diction. Some practitioners encourage patients to write *pathographies* written as part of a three-part chart where patients and physicians write about themselves and their sense of the treatment process and respond to each other's accounting. Applying the process to children can involve drawing, painting, singing, musical instruments, and dance as well as writing.

CONCLUDING REMARKS

To the extent we live our authentic individual stories and prepare children and teens to do the same, we encourage the orderly growth of ourselves and each other.

ഔ COMMENTARY ഔ

CONNECTIONS

More of us live alone than ever (e.g., Klinenberg, 2012) and do so without sacrificing our pack-like instinct to connect with others to feel, safe, protected, and valued. One way we satisfy this primal need is by using the internet to create and foster relationships that satisfy our need for affiliation as some face-to-face ones may do (e.g., Turkle, 2012). And, for those of us with stuttering problems, online social networking provides an expanded and global opportunity to meet, interact with, and learn from and with others who also have stuttering problems. We blog, tweet, and post about our understanding of stuttering problems and our experience having them with others who have stuttering problems and with professionals through *listservs*, facebook pages, *blogs, tweets*, and other internet platforms established primarily for people who wish to share knowledge and expedience with and about stuttering problems. As we listen to podcasts and view TED talks and YouTube uploads addressing the nature and treatment of stuttering problems, we further heighten our knowledge about what we might do to help resolve our problem or that of someone we care about. The sense of recognition and belonging we can feel as members of a relatively small minority locally and world-wide through reaching-out online helps provide some relief from the almost omnipresent anxiety we can feel surrounded by associates, co-workers, family members, and, even, friends who do not share our seemingly idiosyncratic experience of having a stuttering problem. Being with them, we can feel like an outsider, alone and vulnerable.

But we are not an outsider any more than those without stuttering problems are insiders. As Chief Seattle, legendary Suquamish tribal leader; Thich Nhat Hanh, Zen meditation master; Carl Jung, pioneering psychoanalyst; and other wise individuals remind us: There are no insiders, and there are no outsiders. There is just us, connected inextricably to one another. For instance, the lead character of the former CBS dramatic series, *Joan of Arcadia*, fictional teenager Joan Girardi described her group of friends as, ". . . one body with six heads." Or, applying the metaphor used by Buddhists to illustrate the inter-connectiveness of all life forms: Each of us is a strand in the web of life, a jewel in *Indra's net*. Every one of us, whether or not we have a stuttering problem, is part of the whole in which no one can exist separate from the rest and in which no one is more or less important than the rest, ever.

Think of buying a bag of potato chips, a seemingly isolated act. Yet, we need to have the money to do so, which we may have earned working at a particular company, free-lancing, dog-sitting, selling the car we no longer needed or want, etc. Think of all those interpersonal connections. Then, of course, people at the United States Mint had to design and fabricate the coins and paper money we used in the transaction to get the chips. Others, too, such as members of the United States Congress, which approves the design of the money, and the United States Federal Reserve, which maintains the stability of the financial system, also contribute to our ability to purchase the chips and, perhaps, so, too, do the manufacturers who fabricated and formed the plastic we may have used for the purchase and the financial institutions which provided the card to us. And, then there are those who grew, harvested, and transported the potatoes before they were processed into chips and after they were packaged and placed into containers for shipping to wholesale and retail outlets, a process which also includes those who designed the packages and shipping containers and who marketed the product and the brand. The list of those involved in our seemingly simple purchase of a bag of potato chips may be endless.

This quality of connectedness or being, sometimes called *dependent co-arising*, or *inter-being* (e.g., Hahn, 2004), underscores our individual and collective existence, marked by increasing starkness as we now witness fluctuations in the global economy, climate and environmental change, and increasing cultural blandness.

Whatever we who have stuttering problems can do to remember our essential membership in the whole minimizes our occasional or lingering sorrow if we mistakenly think of ourselves as "outsider," diminishing our problem. Listening to and reading fictional stories and biographical or autobiographical accounts of people who confront personal challenges of various kinds and prevail reminds us we, too, have the capacity to face and skillfully move through and past our fears and daunting circumstances, if we choose to do so.

While we may, at times, identify more strongly with those who have stuttering problems and prefer to know and contemplate their stories, especially those which disclose how they have learned or are learning to speak with greater ease, we recognize we also learn much about how to prevail from considering deeply the stories of those who do not have stuttering problems. Their tales elevate us in an exceptionally helpful way. They remind us they are not "The Other," the fortunate ones, unburdened by travail any more than we are "The Other," the unfortunate ones destined to face unrelenting adversity. We recognize, like us, people who do not have or never have had stuttering problems face challenges to be as they wish. They, too, experience fear. They, too, experience betrayal and discouragement. They, too, experience failure. They, too, feel loneliness. And, like them, we, too, can grow strong facing what we fear. We recognize like them we can draw on our capacity to be brave and to persevere to resolve obstacles we encounter working to be as we wish. And we notice, like them, we can experience joy when we prevail. Deeply considering their stories highlights our fundamental sameness which helps release us from the false idea we are separate, different, and apart. And that recognition can bring us, as it can bring anyone who feels alienated, profound relief.

So, putting aside the mistaken belief we are or could be separate from those who do not have stuttering problems, we assume our rightful place within our family, at work, in our faith or spiritual community, and in our local and global communities with confidence. We concentrate on being informed, thoughtful, contributing individuals. And we hone our ability to communicate effectively with ourselves and with one another to add our voice with vigor and humility to that of those around us to enhance this world we share. And through our occasional suffering we can affirm our essential connection with and our responsibility to one another as poetically stated by environmental activist, author, and scholar Joanna Macy (1993),

> *To be able to suffer with is good news because it means you can share power with, share joy with, exchange love with. Let your pain tell you that you are not alone. What we thought might have been sealing us off can become connective tissue.*

5

SHENPA, STUTTERING, AND ME

INTRODUCTION

Not very long ago, after talking with me for approximately 15 minutes, an acquaintance felt compelled to pronounce, *"You need high challenges."* He was right. I do. After all, I chose to abandon a tenured university position to work full-time as a therapist, launch a business without prior business experience, and create a functional method of live theater captioning without training as a captioner. Entrepreneur-type? Well, partially. I'm as complex in my make-up and expression as anyone else, and labels are hit-and-miss as descriptors of me as they are of others. Yet, the one common element of my being throughout the past 25 years has been a dedication to self-improvement. Not that I thought I was a crusty hag needing mellowing or a timorous soul needing to successfully wind my way into society, I just needed to know who I was. Sounds strange, but I was sure I was more than what I seemed. Like many other thinking, curious adults, especially women, I felt, after years of full-time schooling, working, and relating, I had lost touch with me. Oh,

I could name the roles I took on, speech therapist, researcher, professor, wife, mother, ex-wife, boss, artist, and so on, and draw out personal characteristics revealed as I carried them out, or didn't, but that just didn't tell me what I needed to know. So, I set out to learn.

Among the tools I found useful to excavate "me" from the *strata* of conditioned attitudes, feelings, and behaviors I had piled on over the years, like layers of fine gauze encasing a mummy, is the basic meditation technique labeled *mindfulness* (e.g., Hahn, 2000; Kabat-Zinn, 2005, 1990; Langer, 2009; 1989). Applying this method to my quest has provided all I hoped and more. Two years ago, my commitment to the practice led to my awareness of a related one, colloquially referred to as "getting unstuck" (ChÖdrÖn, 2005; 2003). The practice, an ancient one, was developed to manage *shenpa,* a Tibetan word that translates as "hooked." *Shenpa* refers to the experience of having an urge we feel compelled to immediately relieve, like scratching an itch. Upon being hooked, we tense, close down, and withdraw. Then we try to quickly satisfy it. *Shenpa is both the itching and the scratching.* When I perceived that *shenpa,* its nature, the compulsion to react to it, the manner of reacting, and the personal beliefs surrounding it described the root of my stuttering pattern, I literally said, "YES!" to the practice.

This essay outlines my experience dealing with the *shenpa* of my stuttering problem. In the process, I describe my stuttering problem in a bit more detail than I did in a paper prepared for the 6th Annual ISAD Conference (Silverman, 2003). By sharing my experience dealing with *shenpa,* I am not suggesting its adoption by others with or without stuttering problems. In fact, I am not even suggesting that self-directed personal change is necessary. That is a personal decision, of course. What I do want to impart, though, is that I have found working with the *shenpa* of my stuttering to be very hard work, even with prior experience practicing *mindfulness,* and that the results unpredictably follow their own time table. Yet, I have found the changes satisfying and the process even more so.

You may not wish to take up this practice if you find self-analysis annoying and burdensome, but you may want to read this essay to satisfy yourself that stuttering, like over-eating, is " . . . the tip of the iceberg (Sheehan, 1958, p. 123)" and that desirable, successful personal change can be, in part, self-directed.

GETTING STUCK AND GETTING UNSTUCK

The Four Steps

The first step to getting unstuck is *recognizing* the earliest signs of being stuck. For me, I have learned that can involve a sense of being grabbed by the front of the throat and feel like what I imagine being choked by another must feel like. Each time, I am surprised and frightened such that I momentarily stop the mental flow of words I intend to speak. My eyes widen. My torso recoils. I am not here. I am wondering what brought about this ambush and why. I panic wanting to get free. I want to be comfortable. *Shenpa* has hooked me. *I'm stuck. I scratch.* I squeeze my eye and facial muscles and tense my thoracic and abdominal muscles to help push out the words. Immediately, as they begin to sputter out, I feel victorious *and* defeated. I feel elated because I took control of the situation and escaped, but then, in a nanosecond, recognizing I stuttered, I feel sad because I lost control of my body. The shame lasts but a second or so, but the experience adds to my stockpile of perceived personal short-comings. *Shenpa*, 1. Ellen-Marie, 0. Sound familiar?

After Step One, I can apply Steps Two and Three to help get unstuck when I next begin to detect I am being throttled by stuttering.

Step Two is *renouncing* the urge to force words out. That means staying with the tension, the closing down, and the withdrawing and noticing and experiencing whatever feelings and sensations arise and morph while dismissing discursive thoughts about them –- *and not forcing*. To appreciate what is required: The next time you feel you need to sneeze, attend to the feelings and sensations of needing to sneeze, but do not sneeze.

Staying helps break down my customary automatic response. I don't think about being strangled. I release my judgment about the tension. I simply notice all I can about it's physical nature, i.e., where it is, how it feels –- warm, cold, throbbing, etc., how it looks –- its color, size, and so on and my surroundings. My fear melts.

Step Three, involves *relaxing* into the urge to force. I accept, even embrace, the tension with kindness, like a mother comforting her anxious child, rather than display resistance and aversion, reactions that encourage fear. I begin or resume talking when I no longer feel afraid. I say what I want to say. I concentrate on providing information, giving minimal to no thought about making a good impression by not stuttering.

Step Four is *resolving* to apply Steps One through Three for as long as it takes to disrupt my habitual pattern of forcing.

OUTCOME TO DATE

You may consider the process too long to be practical. But the actual time transitioning from Step One through Step Four on any given occasion is extremely brief because I have practiced *mindfulness* for some time. Without that experience, applying the Four-Step Process of Getting Unstuck would be untenable.

But, like others working with *shenpa*, I rarely recognize the tension before I react to quell it (ChÖdrÖn, 2005, 2003). But I usually am able to relax into the desire to force. One thing I do is what I have taught others by providing them a short woven grass tube then instructing them to place one index finger into one end, their other index finger into the other, then remove their fingers from the tube. Most start pulling. Pulling stretches and narrows the tube, squeezing their fingers. Feeling caught, they pull harder. The tube tightens even more. When they stop pulling, they can extract their fingers easily.

Daily, I take time to reflect on my experience stuttering. I approach this time with kindness toward myself, no blame or regret. I consider this a time of learning. After all, that is what I am about, and mistakes offer opportunities to capture key insights so-called successes often do not.

The benefit I most appreciate is the feeling of greater mastery over my thoughts and thought-related behavior. If I perceive laryn-geal constriction, I am no longer overwhelmed. I feel more like a flight controller who alerts a pilot to possible interference and sug-gests options than a pilot encountering turbulence without warn-ing. So far, after slightly less than a year of reasonably dedicated practice, I have not observed changes in the amount or form-type of my stuttering; I still stutter by repeating words and parts of words usually in clusters of three or more (Silverman, 1973). But I struggle less.

I am not so concerned about what others think about how I talk; I am more concerned about what they think about what I say. I believe what you stand for is more important than how you stand and that substance matters more than form. So, I am not distressed that I still stutter about 2 or 3 times on any given day.

Addressing the *shenpa* of my stuttering has shown me that my stuttering is, as Wendell Johnson (1956, p.216-217) postulated, ". . . an anticipatory, apprehensive, hypertonic avoidance reaction." I have become convinced I may stutter to avoid the sensation being grabbed by the neck brings that leads me to fear I will be strangled if I do not contest the throttling. Sometime I may have insights into other provocateurs for my stuttering. Right now, this is what I know.

Where the tension comes from I am not always certain. But I do know that talking with certain people in person or over the telephone seems to occasion the feeling of my imminent strangulation. They are people I know fairly well and people I scarcely know at all. They are people I am talking to for the first time or people I have spoken with before. I feel fear, even terror, in association with each, often before any words are exchanged. This, too, is a form of *shenpa*.

Working with the *shenpa* of my stuttering is not about learning to apply speech controls. It is about noticing what I am experiencing and what I am thinking and doing in relation to that. It is about patience. It is about being aware of choices and selecting ones right for me at the time. It is about greater acceptance of what living brings and of myself. Basically, I envision the practice as parenting. If I want my child to behave appropriately, I need to learn to communicate with my child clearly, consistently, and kindly. Addressing the *shenpa* of my stuttering teaches me to consistently and respectfully send messages to my body that help me communicate with greater ease and satisfaction.

A final benefit from doing this work has been the reminder that the deepest learning comes through experience. Had I accepted this process in theory but not practiced it, I would not have made the changes in outlook and behavior I have for which I am grateful.

I have not had direct access to any teacher or mentor to help me establish and develop my practices. My knowledge of the practices of *mindfulness* and *shenpa* have come through reading and listening to lectures recorded on CD's, DVD's, and video tapes.

CONCLUSION

Actually, I have no final conclusion. I am pleased with benefits I am receiving that I feel derive, at least in part, from the practice, i.e., increased freedom from fear and greater self-discipline, awareness, compassion, and self-acceptance. I intend to continue this combined practice.

ഇ COMMENTARY ഇ

FEAR

Who has not heard that by facing our fears we neutralize their oppressive hold on us. Freeing ourselves from their dark influence that encourages us to expect and accept less for ourselves than we need and deserve opens channels and pathways to liberating growth. If we do not receive this message early in life from caregivers, who recognize their hallowed task as that of preparing us to venture ever farther away from them and into the world at large when we would rather remain where we are, we surely will later on. We may receive it from friends, associates, and family members, who challenge us to be all we can and through personal, work, and community relationships that demand risk-taking from us. And, eventually, we may be the one who gives it to ourselves as we notice that people who face their demons thrive. Seeing them live fully and joyfully while knowing we, who let our fear hold sway over us do not, may help us decide, "I can do this!" and determine we, too, can work through our fear to live more as we wish.

But deciding to skillfully relate to our fear will not of itself change how we respond to it. So-called "good thoughts," as courageous and essential as they are, only bring us to the starting line. We need to move on from there to face our fear to do what we say we wish. And standing at the brink of taking such a journey may give us pause. We may caution ourselves to hold back, saying, "I am too old; I should have begun when I was young" or "I can deal with it; there is no reason to change after all this time," or "Things could be worse," and other similar rationalizations to stay put to spare ourselves the disappointment we would feel if we tried and failed. We surmise the older we are, the more challenging the task may be. And it may, especially for certain fears we want to address. For instance, if we believe we might enjoy the benefits of doing something new for us, such as investing in the stock market or in precious metals, taking up tennis, or becoming a vegan, but doubt we may succeed, we might push ourselves to try after putting into place a safety net to protect ourselves from irreparable harm. If we experience even the slightest bit of encouragement that we are capable of doing what we wish and if we enjoy the activity and its present rewards, such as greater self-knowledge, we probably will continue the process. We have faced our fear head-on and prevailed. We have once again used the tactic we did when we were young to enable us to do something new we found daunting, such as crossing a busy city street on our own, learning to ride a bicycle, or asking someone we liked for a date. We prepped ourselves, made the effort, and felt better about ourselves for trying, especially when we experienced what we wished.

This may have been what our caregivers taught. Like other animals raising their young, they showed us how to be and what to do to survive, even when we did not recognize that is what we needed to learn or feared we might fail trying. They encouraged us to walk when we may not have considered the possibility, take a shower when we feared we might drown from the water running down our face, and attend school even though they realized our anxiety about how well we might perform or fit in made us nauseous. They did all this and more by relentlessly prompting us to take progressive steps to engage ever more fully with people and circumstances beyond our ken, then rewarding us with beaming smiles, conspiratorial nods and winks, loving hugs, high-five's, and other signs meaningful to us, even when we were adults. They wanted us to know they were proud we were living their wish for us: We were fitting in. And we were standing on our own two feet.

But we may receive this message inadvertently, even, perversely. Not all of us experience direction and support from nurturing caregivers or caring family, friends, and associates. Some of us live, work, and, otherwise, engage with those who ridicule our wish and effort to stand on our own two feet. They disparage our success. They do not want us to fit in. These maimed, stunted individuals prefer to bully us for their own amusement. But, if we are fortunate, their taunting, their criticism and worse can push us to listen ever more attentively and consistently to our own inner voice rather than to theirs and to seek and locate guidance from caring and knowledgeable others, who can help us embrace, rather than deny or run from our fear to neutralize its hold on us.

Eventually we learn we do not need to live our fear. We can refuse to succumb to its hi-amp bleat and blare or its seductive whisper that we can neither be more nor do more than we are and have and, if we try, we only will experience pain. We recognize that by setting out on a journey to change we may feel the pain of regret and, even, shame as we encounter and claim long-denied truths about ourselves and others. But we suspect that if we do and if we recognize we did the best we could at the time, the pain we might feel facing the truth about ourselves and others may be less awful and less burdensome than the pain we feel daily by hiding from ourselves and others. And we also imagine this new pain arising from greater awareness may subside quickly, enabling us to move with determination from our previously contracted, bland state into more expansive, vibrant vistas. We no longer feel compelled to live in hopelessness and resentment leading to stagnation.

As we proceed along this path of greater clarity and confidence, we confirm our emergent belief we can be more as we wish. We become bolder, more energetic, and happier. We come to *know* that by acknowledging our fear rather than denying it and by embracing our fear rather than avoiding it, we diffuse it and lessen our pain. But we do not rush the process (e.g., Hanh, 2012). We venture past our stuck point to be and to do more as we wish like a person wading in the shallows of a great lake accommodating to the water temperature while noting the wave action and gauging the current before plunging in for a swim. We emerge from our cocoon of fear in an orderly and prudent manner.

Similarly, we choose to face our fear of stuttering in an orderly manner. We choose to accommodate our stuttering rather than to follow our impulse to eliminate or suppress it and relinquish our desire to instantaneously have our way with it. We accept rather than contend with our fear. We relate to our stuttering the way we would our beloved child when he throws a tantrum. We calmly abide until he accepts our consolation rather than struggling with him to immediately stop and be and do as wish. Otherwise, he probably would intensify and prolong his distressing behavior. Likewise, we calmly abide with our stuttering; otherwise, we will do what we always have done, even as we are trying to put into action well-meaning tactics, such as telling ourselves or reminding ourselves, "Stuttering is OK. Struggling is not." We will struggle to not struggle and, possibly, stutter fiercely, strengthening the lingering doubt we can speak with greater ease more consistently while dampening our resolve to change. Unless and until we learn to quiet our mind and body as we experience fear so we can calmly abide in its presence to take action that helps us relate skillfully to it, we will accomplish no more than that. But we can. This is the message of working with *shenpa*. This seemingly counter-intuitive manner of relating to our fear in the moment by accepting it as *what is* and by renouncing our inclination to contend with and master it to relax into it instead leads us to make helpful choices and skillfully implement related actions that neutralize it. And, as we do all that, we inevitably come to speak with greater ease and satisfaction.

6
MIND MATTERS

Stuttering is the natural eloquence of the fallen.

-- Eugene O'Neill, *Long Day's Journey Into Night*

The righteous fall seven times and seven times rise again.

-- Paraphrase of an *Hasidic* saying

It's not what you're given but what you make of what you're given.

-- Elaine Stritch, Actress

If you're given a lemon, make lemonade.

-- Anonymous

INTRODUCTION

Do not be concerned. I have not written this paper to convince you as someone who has a stuttering problem or cares about someone who does that a stuttering problem is a glorious gift. That is your decision entirely, and I have not written this paper to persuade you to adopt one view or another about that. But I would like you to consider how differently you might feel and how differently you might live if you thought your stuttering problem was a gift from how differently you might feel and how differently you might live if you believed it was, at best, a burden.

What we believe about ourselves, the world, and our place in it decidedly affects how we live and whether we find life to be a source of joy or suffering. Psychiatrist Eric Berne, the founder of Transactional Analysis, built his theory of personality and method of psychotherapy around this single idea, an idea that also ordered the work of other notable psychiatrists and psychologists, such as the founders of psychoanalysis and cognitive-behavioral psychotherapy. You may be surprised that mystics and physicists, especially those specializing in the field of quantum physics, share the same idea, that our beliefs shape our reality. Albert Einstein, who asserted *we experience what we believe*, reportedly stressed that the most important question each of us has to answer for ourselves is whether we live in a friendly or a hostile environment. He invited us to consider whether we believe we live in supportive circumstances where our needs are fully met or in a culture of scarcity that creates "Have's" and "Have-Not's" and requires us to struggle to attain what we feel is rightfully ours.

The Tibetan Buddhist nun and master teacher Pema Chödrön (2005a) generously offers an anecdote from her own meditation practice to illustrate how personal beliefs may influence the process of cultivating personal change. A North American, who writes and lectures on meditation practices, including working with *shenpa* (Silverman, 2005), she discussed her experience relating to deep anxiety while attending a retreat for approximately one week. Throughout, she remained present with what she described as a wordless anxiety, neither denying nor suppressing it, while applying various meditation techniques to soften and melt it away. But she could not budge it. She presented this, to her, troubling challenge to her teacher Dzigar Kongtrul Rinpoche, who provided some relief by acknowledging, that he, too, had had just such an experience. He related that, for him, the experience had lasted months and had been a good teacher. Encouraged, she continued working with the feeling. One day her teacher appeared during her meditation practice as she was struggling.

"Oh, I know that feeling," he announced. "That's the *Dakini Bliss!*"

"*Dakini Bliss*?" Pema pondered excitedly. "Oh, Wow! Right! The feeling does have the intensity of bliss," she rhapsodized.

She then became eager to continue experiencing the feeling, but it was gone. From that, she realized she had been subconsciously considering what she thought was a sense of anxiety as something bad. And, because she believed she was experiencing something bad, she struggled against it. And because she believed she was experiencing something bad, she considered herself bad because she was having a bad experience, and she struggled with herself. When her teacher's words reframed the discomforting experience, she re-imaged the feeling as desirable and herself as good, even special. She transformed her response to the experience and to herself from shame and guilt and, possibly, anger and resentment to exuberant acceptance. She even longed to re-experience the feeling. She ceased all struggle to dispel it. She, in fact, welcomed the experience as a valued guest. Once she did that, it disappeared. She quickly understood why. She knew surrendering to, even embracing, what seems undesirable is a central activity of certain mindfulness practices (e.g., Chödrön, 2003; Hahn, 2000; 2004) and a requirement for what the eminent Swiss psychoanalysis pioneer Carl Jung labeled as personal individuation, i.e., experiencing wholeness by recognizing, embracing, and, finally, integrating our own shadow. As Abraham Lincoln cautioned, "A house divided against itself can not stand."

Our beliefs about stuttering and ourselves contribute to the formation of stuttering problems, their continuance, and, ultimately, the release from them. Consider the following brief, vignettes:

King George VI of England

Because he developed a stuttering problem as a child, King George IV, who lived in a culture that considered people with stuttering problems edgy, inconsequential, and "just that way," felt doomed to stutter and fall short as a communicator. Those beliefs weighed heavily on him. Despite trying at various times to overcome his stuttering problem, he never did.

Tiger Woods

Tiger Woods described himself during a March 26, 2006, interview with Ed Bradley on CBS's "60 Minutes" as a shy child who stuttered. When asked how he overcame his stuttering problem, he replied, "I went to school. I worked my butt off. I talked to my dog. He fell asleep. But I didn't stutter all over myself any more." Even then he demonstrated a "mind over matter" approach.

Each seemed to experience stuttering as he believed possible. King George VI as victim, Tiger Woods as victor. They are no different than we; we, too, live what we believe. That is why I have spent the past two and one-half decades deciding what to believe and noting whether or not I was living as I intended.

PERSONAL BELIEFS

As a graduate student in speech pathology at the University of Iowa enrolled in a course in general semantics (Korzybski, 1955), I learned to identify what the instructor, O.T. Bontrager, called *certainties*. He believed certainties, or basic beliefs, spawned our behavior and that most were unconscious. He reasoned that if we excavated the beliefs leading to our problems then eliminated or altered them, based on current knowledge and experience, we would lead happier, more fulfilling lives. To demonstrate that, he instructed us to analyze one personal situation weekly during the semester that led to feelings of unpleasantness to determine which belief or beliefs led to those feelings. We started by verbalizing our irritation then repeatedly asking "Why?" I have used this brilliant method ever since, most recently after stuttering more severely than ever one afternoon two weeks ago. You may think you know all you need to know about "attitudes" and "attitude modification" and their relationship to stuttering, but this simple yet penetrating method can yield striking and helpful results. Let me demonstrate.

First, Some Background: On a recent Friday, just before 5 o'clock p.m., I bit into a chocolate wafer and experienced the lingual surface of a bicuspid fall away. I called my dentist immediately and was told by the receptionist that, since I was experiencing no pain, I would have to wait until the coming Monday to be seen. That Monday, to my surprise and horror, the dentist informed me I needed a root canal. As I waited for the local anesthetic to take effect, already mentally numbed-out by hearing how much the procedure cost, my body could not have been more tense. I was close to hyperventilating as my fear of facing impending, improbable pain overtook me. To divert myself, I decided to ask the dentist waiting on my right a question about the procedure. But my mind, concentrating more on imminent pain, performed poorly as an expressive language generator. Nevertheless, I launched the string of words supposed to be the question by tensely repeating their initial sounds and syllables. I can not remember the words I was trying to say, but I can remember vividly the incomparable extreme tension I experienced in my thorax, throat, mouth, and face as I began stuttering while being astonished both by the force of my stuttering and by noticing me tell myself, *"Let it go. Let the stuttering be what it wants to be. Let it come out."* Hearing advice at that time and that advice in particular strongly caught my attention.

So, to my credit and the result of a several year and continuing *shenpa* practice (Silverman, 2005), which teaches acknowledging uncomfortable experience, refraining from acting compulsively and habitually to escape it, and relaxing into the urge to escape, I did what I told myself to do. Yet my stuttering was more explosive and involved more consecutive words than ever. Although my eyes were directed toward my lap, I sensed the sitting postures of the dentist and the technician sitting on my left change from relaxed to stiff. They seemed to be barely breathing. I felt stunned, puzzled, and profoundly embarrassed to act so out-of-control. Once the dentist began the root canal work, I noticed my whole body, particularly my thorax, behave uncharacteristically. I hyperventilated. I white-knuckled the chair arms. I sweated, especially across my forehead. And I screamed fluently.

Applying the Technique. Later that evening when the anesthetic had worn off and I felt composed, I checked out was behind my surprising personal-worst/personal-best stuttering by asking and answering *WHY?* My first response was: *I wasn't able to get my thoughts together.* To a subsequent *WHY?*, I replied: *I was fearful. My fear was so strong it overpowered my ability to think and disrupted necessary coordination between breathing and speaking. WHY? Because I did not breathe evenly from my deep abdominal area to keep my mind calm and incisive; I let the fear overwhelm me, making my breathing shallow and irregular. WHY? Because I have not yet established the practice of even, deep abdominal breathing at all times. WHY? Because, when I heard of it, I understood why and how to do it, felt I could easily do it, and thought I did not need to practice. I believed I could "turn it on" when I felt strong emotion cloud my thinking. I did not fully take into account the speed and power of strong emotion to disrupt cognitive control of my behavior.* So, here was my primary belief: *If I understand what I need to do, I do not need to practice.* And me –- a therapist! I had to both laugh and wince at the truthfulness of that discovery.

Like me, you may find verbalizing your actual, not professed, core beliefs embarrassing at first. You may think, *"I know better."* and get angry, even depressed. But be kind. Pat yourself on the back. Celebrate! You discovered an unhelpful belief. Now you can modify your thinking; establish a new, helpful mind-body link; and grow. Wonderful! And do not forget to tap into your sense of humor to enliven the experience!

CODA

Since we mind our minds, we need to know what they are telling us. So, if we want to know what beliefs we are living, we need to take time to carefully analyze our words and actions. Like F. M. Alexander, the orator, who cured himself of chronic laryngitis by changing the way he thought when initiating action then founded *The Alexander Technique*, we, too, can become more like we were meant to be by recognizing what we deeply believe.

✂ COMMENTARY ✂

KINDNESS

Nowhere can personal change become more easily upended than the moment we discover it is we who have been causing grief for ourselves by living an out-dated, ill-suited, subconscious belief we first adopted as a child or teen. As the clouds that had been covering our eyes suddenly and, often, unexpectedly part to reveal our folly, we may see ourselves as I did, an apparition — a lumbering adult body ridden by a strident three-year-old perched atop my shoulders ordering me around.

This startling image depicts how many of us, whether or not we have a stuttering problem, may live. We may be 20 or 30 years old with a high school or college education yet living according to the now subconscious beliefs about stuttering we fashioned when we were three or four and confirmed when we were 10 or so using our limited experience and immature cognitive skills to make decisions about how we need to be to survive as someone who stutters. We may believe stuttering might kill us quickly by strangulation as we stutter or slowly if our stuttering so displeases our caregivers that they abandon us, forcing us to fend for ourselves in a world that shows little comfort or mercy to orphans with limited knowledge, skills, and means. To survive, we may decide we need to escape from our stutter, which can thrust us into a blind panic encouraging us to internally and externally thrash about struggling to free ourselves so that we can breathe. Or, trying to prevent ourselves from being detected as someone who stutters, we may decide we need to squeeze and push out words and speech sounds or hold them back before someone can notice we are stuttering. And, perhaps, most harmful of all to ourselves we may choose to be silent rather than to talk and risk stuttering, even though we recognize that by being mute we may not get what we want or we may be thought of as unintelligent.

Even though we have been stuttering for 10 or 20 years or more and are very much alive and, perhaps, fortunate enough to share life with a beloved partner, parent children we cherish, work enough to satisfy our needs and, even, some of our desires, and enjoy life in other meaningful ways, subconsciously we may continue to believe stuttering may finish us off at any time. Why else would we still fear and try to avoid or cover-up stuttering with such determination and ferocity. We have amassed ample and conspicuous experience to prove we can stutter and survive. Yet those of us with stuttering problems continue to live in fear of stuttering.

The chagrin we feel as we recognize we are living as our young self, believing stuttering can kill us or harm us substantially, rather living as the adult we are according to what we currently know to be true can hit us hard in the gut. Metaphorically, we crumple and crumble and can sink into a hole we can enlarge into a pit if we allow our embarrassment to become despair by mercilessly attacking ourselves for living unconsciously. We may think no one else could be as ignorant or as foolish as we to live according to a preschooler's or teen's world view. Yet what we do not realize is that everyone except, perhaps, mystics and saints live as unconsciously as we have been by acting-out beliefs we develop as young children. This is a tendency some, such as psychoanalysts Alfred Adler and Eric Berne, refer to as *scripting*, or creating a story we reactively act-out instead of living freshly and authentically moment-by-moment. They and others have encouraged us to uncover the beliefs which form the basis of our personal scripts if we wish to consistently experience more of what we wish and less of what we do not, such as communicating confidently and fearing stuttering, respectively. They assure us as did Jesus The Christ in The Gnostic

Gospels (e.g., Pagels, 1989) that what we uncover about ourselves will free us and that what we fail to uncover can destroy us. Pioneering psychoanalyst Carl Jung refers to this great task as getting to know our psyche, which he and his esteemed colleague Marie-Louise von Franz referred to as the *individuation process* (von Franz, 1964).

This process may take some time as we work our way through the anger we feel that we often suppress through denial and then express through self-recrimination critical of our discovery we have been unconsciously living out an unhelpful belief or two that twisted us. As we acknowledge what we recognize to be true, that we literally have been acting childishly, we often feel shame and, perhaps, remorse. Our embarrassment may be so strong and our perceived resources seem so limited that we may refuse to increase our discomfort by considering changing because we do not wish to so publically acknowledge our folly and, perhaps, because we believe we can not change to be more as we wish. Or we may conclude our lives are set. So, we may continue as we have, increasing our unhappiness.

But, as we open to learning what psychology tells us about being an adult, we realize we have lived as most do. That is sad; but it is also true. Feeling angry and, perhaps, ashamed about how we have lived does not change that reality, but feeling gratitude for our discovery or reminder that we are like others can help us change. And so can becoming informed of our options for change as we apply our newly adopted certainties about how to live well. Knowing what we have been doing and why makes clear the basic choice we now have: We can choose to speak and live more as we wish or we can continue to struggle and feel alienated. And, if we choose to change, we benefit from accepting the suggestion made by an Italian tutor to his pupil, writer Elizabeth Gilbert, played by Julia Roberts in the movie *Eat Pray Love* (Salt and Murphy, 2010), based on Gilbert's solo journey as a 30-something through Italy, India, and Bali to discover the truth of who she was. We should be, the tutor explained, " . . . very polite with our-selves when we learn something new." We, too, recognize being kind and gentle with ourselves, which differs from self-indulgence (e.g., Salzberg, 2011), invokes the clarity of mind, the strength of conviction, the patience, and the encouragement needed for us to make helpful decisions about how we wish to live from now on and to see them through.

7

CREATING CONDITIONS
FOR CHANGE

I hope you will find something helpful in the thoughts I share about *Change*, something we all long for, dread, and deal with daily in one way or another. After 43 years of working with this process as a professional and more than that as an individual, I find I am just beginning to understand what is involved. And I am impressed by the courage and patience required.

INTRODUCTION

Those of us who seek to change the way we communicate or to help someone else do that are the intended audience. What binds us together in common cause is the challenge to manage change in a manner that is liberating. I know for sure that relating well to change bolsters the process and that not doing so causes it to falter, even implode. What follows stems from my experience of what is necessary, what is helpful, and what is involved.

71

DEATH, TAXES, AND CHANGE

Wherever and whenever we are born and into what circumstance, among the basic elements of life we share are these: We die. We pay taxes. And we deal with change. Since we arrived in this world fresh from our mother's body, we have changed. Our bodies changed. They grew longer, wider, thicker. They grew whiskers. They grew bald. Our interests changed. No longer amused by lying on our back and sucking our toes, we rolled over and crawled. We listened to stories and songs, then wrote them. We longed to become an astrophysicist until we discovered *croissants* and fancied becoming a *chefs de cuisine*. Our thoughts about ourselves changed, too, from rapt attention during infancy to anxious assessment during childhood and beyond as we learned to compare our features, skills, and experiences with others and began wondering, *"Am I Good Enough?"* And, quite often, from then on, we thought we were not. We were too tall, too thin, too quiet, too awkward, too dumb, too poor, and so on. We wanted to fit in, maybe *"WOW"* our friends. We wanted to change.

Sometimes we did not know we needed to change, but our parents did. They may have decided we needed to stop stuttering, which, often, we did not know we were doing until they, or a relative, or the parent of a friend, or, maybe, a neighbor across the hall, or a classroom teacher said something to us such as, *"That was smooth. Cool!" "Slow down!" "Easy!"* We were quick to pick up we had to talk better to please those powerful people. We needed to change.

EXPERIENCES LAST

Before you ask someone to change the world, make sure they like it the way it is.

- - - Vin Diesel, actor

I sometimes think there is nothing as durable as childhood experiences. They color our lives as they shape them. The murky interaction of our individual temperaments with our early experience as interpreted by our maturing cognitive apparatus establishes what we come to believe as true about ourselves, others, and the world (e.g., Chess and Thomas, 2005) and sets the stage for how we think, feel, and act from then on (e.g., Steiner, 1994) unless and until we recreate our individual cosmology. As a personal example, nothing influenced me more than my mother's death when I was three and one-half.

These are the basic facts:

Late at night, the first day home from the hospital after delivering my sister *via* c-section, my mother began retching. The unfamiliar sounds first awakened then frightened me. I put on my slippers and ran into my parents' bedroom just across the hall. When I entered, I saw my mother lying on the far side of the double bed on her right side, her right arm cradling a white coated bucket. She and I were the only ones there. She lifted her head and held me with her eyes. They seemed larger than ever. Fear and love radiating from them held me in silence. She did not speak.

I was terrified. I had never seen my mother, my protector, weak and helpless. She resumed retching. My terror increased as I helplessly watched her body convulse and heard, once again, those wrenching sounds. More than anything, I wanted her to stop. I wanted her to be herself. Not knowing what else to do, I jumped up and down, up and down, shouting, *"Shut-up. Shut-up."* Almost immediately, my father appeared. He quickly and tenderly carried me from their bedroom. Within moments, he prepared a place for us to sleep together on the living room floor, a few feet from their bedroom door. Early the next morning, he went in to check on her.

Then the awful screaming began. She was dead. She had died from a hemorrhagic stroke while we slept.

These are my three and one-half year-old self's interpretations of those facts:

Words kill. I killed my mother with my words.

I am a bad person.

I am alone.

I do not deserve to be loved ever again.

This is what I told myself and no one else at the time. And that is what I repeated to myself every now and again for many years thereafter whenever I experienced something that reminded me of that original experience. For instance, when I was 10 and in the fifth grade, our beloved principal, who looked and walked like a gracefully aging *prima* ballerina, uncharacteristically visited our class. She came to scold us. She warned us that no one was ever to say to anyone else the worst words that could be said.

The words she banned in the classroom and forbade on the school yard were *Shut-up!* Shocked, I immediately flashed back to the night I shouted those very same words at my mother then never saw her again. I heard our principal say more, but I did not listen to her words. I was acknowledging to myself I was as bad as I thought. I was deeply ashamed. I felt I was sinking. Eventually, I no longer remembered the words of my interpretations. But they already had set patterns of perception and behavior into motion that colored my entire life until I recalled them several decades later and challenged them kindly but firmly using my adult knowledge and experience.

Nevertheless, the beliefs they fostered that I was horrid and unworthy of love and that spoken words can kill still emit silent sprouts that I continue to toil at uprooting.

This particular example may be unique, but the tendency to interpret experience is not. It is common-place for all of us, children and adults. And, in fact, it is our interpretation of what we experience that affects us more so than the experience itself (e.g., Chess and Thomas, 2005; Steiner, 1994). For children, interpretations are especially noteworthy. First, because children lack the knowledge, experience, and capacity to draw the measured conclusions an adult might. And Secondly, the conclusions children draw have far-reaching consequences for how they live their lives from then on.

We need to take this into account when we arrange to have a child tested or enrolled in speech therapy. Children's generally unspoken interpretations of why they are having new experiences and what those experiences mean, what they have to do be successful in them, and how they need to be to be accepted and, thereby, survive all need to be seriously considered. While we may never exactly know their interpretations of testing or therapy experiences, we can be certain they are making them, e.g., *Jason's Secret* (Silverman, 2001). Therefore, to paraphrase Vin Diesel, the actor quoted at the start of this section,

Before we ask children to change, let's be sure to first teach them to love themselves just as they are.

If we do that, their self-worth will be based on who they are, not on what they do, how they do it, or what they have, and they will have a good chance to live genuinely happy, satisfying lives. *If we teach them to love themselves*, they will seek the best for themselves and strive to have it. *If we teach them to love themselves,* they will do all that is necessary to materialize the change they want, if and when they decide to change how they look, act, or think. And *If we teach them to love themselves,* they can love.

PENTIMENTO

. . . pentimento . . . a change of mind . . . a way of seeing and then seeing again.

- - - Lillian Hellman, Playwright, Author (1973)

At some point in our lives, we may come to feel stuck. We find that although we have changed our jobs we experience the same relationships with co-workers and supervisors we detested before. We notice that even when we align with new partners we experience the same unpleasant "push-pull" relationship we had with so many others before. We join a different faith community only to feel the need to fend off fellow worshippers behaving as annoyingly intrusive as the ones in the faith community we left behind. And, despairingly, we may observe that our stuttering problem is no better or worse than it was years earlier despite our fervent desire and, occasional, intense efforts to rid ourselves of it. If we want to change what we experience, we come to realize, we will have to change at the most basic level.

During my undergraduate clinical training in stuttering problems, I encountered a woman with a stuttering problem who had achieved a certain notoriety at our university speech clinic. She, someone in her mid-30's who worked as a secretary in a large firm, had learned each of Van Riper's various stuttering control techniques. She would proudly demonstrate her mastery of their mechanics behind closed doors in treatment but nowhere else because, in her words, *"They don't feel natural."* Marcy, not her real name, showed that changing the mechanics of speech is not synonymous with personal change, although it can certainly lead to that.

Those of us with stuttering problems come to know changing how we talk then changing how we communicate can change our lives. And, as paradoxical as it first may seem, we sometimes choose to keep our lives just as they are even though doing so means continuing to experience the fear, shame, and embarrassment of

76

stuttering we detest because, fundamentally, we are comfortable (e.g., Myss, 1998). Although our lives, like everyone else's, are not always pleasant, they are fairly predictable. We've got them under control, at least most of the time. And that is what so many of us crave, especially in these uncertain times. We want to know where we will be having breakfast today, what we'll be doing Sunday morning, where we will shop Friday after work, when we will be vacationing, and so on. If we change how we communicate, we will change how we live. We may change jobs. We may change relationships. We may change locales. The winds of change may transport us to a very different life gradually or swiftly. We can not be sure. That is why change requires courage and endurance, the courage to let go of the past to move into an uncertain future along an unknown path and the commitment to take the ride as far as it goes for as long as it takes. As long as we prefer the comfort of the known over the risk of the unknown, we will not sincerely work for the change we say we would like to have.

We will change, nevertheless. That is inevitable. We will become both more and less like we currently are. Our habits will grow stronger until our physical and, perhaps, our mental capacities will grow weaker. Our circumstances will change. Friends and loved ones will move away. Some will die. New people will become important. Work outside the home will change or end. We may develop hobbies that engage us. Nothing about us will stay the same except, perhaps, for a while, our perceptions of how our life is and should be. Until we change them, we will fundamentally live as we have until the very end (e.g., Byrne, 2006; Chess and Thomas, 2005; Hellman, 1973; Myss, 1998; Silverman, 2006; Steiner, 1994). Remember:

A foolish consistency is the hob-goblin of little minds,
adored by little statesmen and philosophers.

- - - Ralph Waldo Emerson, "Self-Reliance" in *Essays,*
Second Series (1847)

෨ COMMENTARY ෨

INTENT

We may say we ought to change. We would be more successful. We would earn more money. We would enjoy more respect from others. But do we *want* to change? That is what we need to know before committing to learning new ways to help ourselves change and aligning with new people to guide us through the process. We need to know our real intent, which may not be what we think it is, if we are to wisely spend our time and our resources to enhance our lives. Otherwise, we may enter arrangements that eventually disappoint us and encourage use to falsely conclude or strengthen the belief we already may hold that we are unable to be and do as we wish.

In Judaism, spiritual leaders place great emphasis on *kavanah,* or intent. They believe *kavanah*, setting the heart prior to reciting a prayer or performing a sacred ritual, elevates the act so that the desired outcome may be realized more completely. They discovered that if the heart is not engaged in the process, the outcome may be shoddy, incomplete, and disappointing. In fact, certain of the wisdom writings in Judaism, for instance the *Pirket Avot* translated as, *The Wisdom of Our Fathers*, advise that preparing to pray by clearing and steadying our minds and hearts is more important than the act of prayer itself. Lacking clear intent, our prayer can become too diffuse to create the effect we desire or for us to realize it has. Those who practice Judaism, especially within the orthodox tradition, often apply the spirit of *kavanah* to all acts of daily life and perform them in mindfulness.

Similarly, introspection can illuminate our true motivation for undertaking activities of ordinary life, such as speaking. Spending time reflecting helps us those of us with stuttering problems discern whether or not and when we want to take the time and shoulder the cost financially, socially, and emotionally of learning to speak with greater ease. Only if we reflect, will we know whether or not we want to work to change how we speak and communicate and how and when we want to do so. We may learn we want to change how we live by changing how we speak or by doing something else, such as seeking a different job, preparing for a different career, ending an unsatisfactory personal relationship, seeking a life partner, expanding a hobby, and in other ways. We may learn we are not now ready to do the actual work of changing how we speak and communicate, but we want to and can begin to pave the way for doing so when we are ready by learning about options available to us and the requirements of each. We may learn we prefer to keep our outer circumstances as they are but change our relationship to them from avoidance and struggle, punctuated by grousing and carping silently or overtly, to non-resistance. Or we may learn we do not want to change what think or do now or, possibly, ever. We do not believe making the effort will help us become happier than we already are.

Self-reflection reduces the likelihood we will burn-up our precious allotment of time in activities that only seem to deepen our unhappiness as we stumble along uncertain of where to go and anxious about what to do to increase our happiness. But we usually deflect the suggestion we take time to reflect. We say that we do not have time, especially if we consciously or subconsciously do not wish to confront what we may need to acknowledge to change. If that is what we tell ourselves, we are saying we do not have the time to undertake a program of change.

So what is our intent? Is it to change to satisfy ourselves? Is it to change to satisfy another? Or is our intent to keep on living as we are, even though we dislike living as we do, because we prefer what we know to what we have yet to experience should we remove some or all of the accouterments that we realize serve as fetters keeping us from experiencing the fullness of our dreams? The choice is ours. There is no right decision and there is no wrong decision when made with deliberation and care. There is only living with intention and purpose or in confusion and anxiety. And there is no need to express our intent to anyone but ourselves. We only need to know it and to live it faithfully for as long as it serves us.

8
HAPPILY EVER AFTER

INTRODUCTION

I'm more fluent than ever; I should feel happy.

*I've been accepted to graduate school by my first choice;
I should feel happy.*

*My child is participating in classroom discussions and making
friends; I should feel happy.*

BUT I DON'T!

Isn't that the way! We get what we want, and, for a while, we are happy. Then we discover what we received does not perfectly match what we expected. And, *Poof!* Anger, sadness, or fear replaces our happiness. Consider:

1. We stutter as fiercely and as much or more than ever days after an amazingly fluent weekend in a fluency workshop, and we crumble for a time. Although we soon resume passably fluent speech, we no longer feel confident interacting because a nagging doubt about whether we will ever be truly fluent drags us down.

2. When we arrive on campus as a new grad student, we discover that continuing grad students are closed and shun friendly contacts with new students. A sharp ache in the pit of our stomach quickly replaces the excitement we felt thinking about socializing with fellow students. We don't want to be part of such a cold culture, but, for financial reasons, we see no other choice but to stay

   AND

3. Our child stutters as much as ever, sometimes more tensely, now that he is making presentations, participating in discussions, and playing with friends. Our anxiety about whether therapy will work for him and whether we enrolled him in the right program replaces the elation we felt when he began opening up.

We could discuss why it is that reverting from happy to sad in each instance is unnecessary, but I selected these examples for another purpose, i.e., to pose the question, *Can we experience lasting happiness?* I think many of us quietly ponder this possibility from time-to-time because we know the hope, indeed, the expectation that we can drives us to enter therapy, to apply to the best graduate programs, to carefully consider decisions for our children, and to make each and every choice count has not yet resulted in everlasting happiness. Sometimes we even may slip into despair, doubting that happiness is for us, concluding it is only for others. From personal experience, I know how easy it is to think this way. I grew up believing what fairy tales taught: If you thought good thoughts and did good deeds, someone or something would rescue you from your bitter situation to live "Happily Ever After." Some years ago, I realized just how strongly that belief affected me when, alone and deeply distressed about facing a series of troubling circumstances, I surprised myself by shouting out to the ether, *"I want my 'Happily Ever After!'"* Frustrated after decades of patterning my life after fairy tale heroines who received the gift of happiness everlasting while I did not, my roar was a bit like the Seinfield character Mr. Costanza, George's father, bellowing, *"Serenity Now!"* when he could not bear feeling undone one second longer. Examining the beliefs I held that lead to that startling reaction helped put me on The Path of Happiness, which I have determinedly traveled since. So, my response to the question, based on knowledge and personal experience, is a definite, *"Yes!"* We can conduct ourselves in a way to be genuinely happy (e.g., Kornfield, 2008: Seligman, 2004) most of the time. Here's how.

NOW OR NEVER

Be happy now! There is no need to wait until therapy fixes us, or we become a certified clinician, or our child no longer stutters. And most of us know it is futile to depend on a fairy godmother or handsome prince to *happify* us. So, if we wait until we and everything we care about are just as we wish, happiness will forever elude us. We will be one speech hesitancy, one clinical certification requirement, or one stuttering episode away. But we do not have to live like that. We have the capacity to be happy right where we are no matter how dire the circumstance, not by relenting or settling but by altering our view, and we possess the power to do so once we realize that. For instance, centuries ago, British poet Richard Lovelace wrote from prison, *"Stone walls do not a prison make, nor iron bars a cage;"* and, last century, *logotherapy* founder, psychiatrist Viktor Frankl (2006) recounted that he survived Nazi concentration camp internment by embracing two thoughts which gave him happiness, rejoining his wife and completing a technical manuscript. Others, informed by their knowledge of sacred texts and personal experience, e.g., Tolle, (2005), Hanh (2004), and Myss (1997), also assert it only is in the present where we can experience happiness. As Loretta La Roche (1995), humor therapist, reminds us, *"The past is history. The future is a mystery. Now is a gift. That's why it's called The Present."*

Pema Chödrön (2006) and other students of human happiness, including Tsultrim Allione (2008) and Martin Seligman (2004), teach us to create enduring happiness for ourselves that can accommodate life's up's and down's, including periods of grief and loneliness, by accepting both "agreeable and disagreeable" as they appear in our lives. For most, doing so initially is contrary to our more instinctive response of resisting what we do not want and doggedly chasing after what we think will remove or lessen our pain. But, by resisting our unpleasant thoughts, feelings, and sensations as we stutter and others' real and imagined negative responses as we do, many of us have layered our stuttering problems with throbbing complexity. As the late Wendell Johnson (1956) cautioned more than a half century ago, a stuttering problem is *". . . an anticipatory, apprehensive, hypertonic avoidance reaction. . . "* and, as such, thrives on resistance. In addition to feeding our stuttering problem, resistance delays our opportunity to learn from carefully studying how we think, act, and feel as we stutter to discern which mind-sets and behaviors we need to release and which to cultivate to speak with increasing ease and finesse. And, by welcoming, rather than resisting, stuttering, as paradoxical as such a choice seems until we do it, we gain enhanced self-esteem (Silverman, 2005).

It is hard to imagine anyone who dwells on what makes them unhappy about the way they speak and about themselves as a speaker benefiting much from speech therapy, unless and until they discover what also makes them happy about how they speak and themselves as speakers. As actor, writer, director, and producer Vin Diesel succinctly stated:

Before you ask someone to save the world,
make sure they like it just the way it is.

Seeing ourselves broadly as we actually function, i.e., as partners, brothers, sisters, fathers, mothers, friends, colleagues, gardeners, community members, etc. demonstrating our individual strengths and weakness rather than through the tightly closed, smudged window of labels, such as female, Jew, Latina, senior citizen, stutterer, and, especially, PWS, (acronym for person who stutters), which diminish our perception of who we are and what we can do for ourselves and others is a good place to start. Therapy and self-help groups which anchor us in a larger, more realistic personal perspective than labels allow are likely to stimulate and support healing because such an orientation is apt to help us think well of ourselves (e.g., Hanh, 2004).

KINDNESS

When we think we deserve to be happy, we treat ourselves kindly. Many of us, after experiencing stuttering-related hurt, choose to be "nice" people. We appear agreeable and encouraging in public, but, in private, especially during our almost continuous self-talk, denigrate ourselves for failing to live up to our standards with associates, family, friends, and strangers because we stuttered or because we believed we squandered an opportunity to be helpful or for personal advancement through our fear of stuttering. This sort of self-abasement that can readily lead to unnecessary disengagement from others (e.g., Silverman, 2003; 2006b) contributes to a mix of dreary and miserable feelings while strengthening stuttering-related avoidant behaviors (e.g., Allione, 2008). Like the legendary French chanteuse Edith Piaf, who lived so challenging a life that she died at 47 appearing years older, yet came to resonate with one of her signature songs, *"No. No Regrets!"* we, too, gain nothing useful by burdening ourselves with feelings of regret and blame. When we release self-recrimination for stuttering, perhaps, we can relate kindly to ourselves. That is when we will find more of the contentment we seek.

CAUTION

Treading a Path of Happiness is not easy. Far from it! Doing so requires commitment to change, i.e., embarking on a journey which can take us we know not where; willingness to take personal responsibility for our choices; and application of honesty and courage, as much as we can muster, moment-by-moment. Some spiritual teachers (e.g., Gimian, 2008, p. 76) advise students, *"It is better not to begin such a journey, but, if you begin, you should go all the way to the destination."* I believe it is more difficult to suffer without knowing a way out than to face unknown challenges. So, I have chosen to walk the path rather than wander in the wilderness. For now, that brings enough reward.

ഔ COMMENTARY ഔ

TRUE HAPPINESS

Have you heard of *The Happy Stutterer*? *Happy Stutterer* is a tag some derisively apply to those who stutter with aplomb. Stuttering seems to have no hold on them. If they stutter, they stutter. If they do not, they do not. Neither outcome seems to faze them. They do not feel angry and depressed when they stutter. And they do not feel elated when they do not. They say what they want at any time, at anyplace, and to anyone without giving thought to whether or not they may stutter. They communicate to communicate rather than to perform stutter-free. This stance brings approval from those who champion their willingness to stutter freely without remorse and without concern and censure from those who believe people should stutter only rarely, as inconspicuously as possible, and, preferably, in private. But Happy Stutterers, being free souls, operate independent of others' beliefs. They follow internal direction. They attend to their own and others' needs for validation, information, and guidance and accept stuttering as a peripheral aspect of speaking that holds no more significance to them than a hiccup. They live with equanimity. Happy Stutterers are on the road to *true happiness.*

By contrast, those of us who fear stuttering are not. We live anxiously. We fret that stuttering when making a phone call, giving a presentation, interviewing for a job, offering a toast at a wedding, and at other times paints us as less intelligent, competent, and authoritative than someone who does not stutter. We fret that we may experience rejection searching for a life partner or trying to satisfy other personal desires, such as traveling solo, adopting children, or operating a small business, because we may come across as unstable because we stutter. And, perhaps, most tragically, we may fret that God, Himself or Herself, may dismiss our prayers or refuse us entrance to "Heaven" because stuttering brands us as fools or as reprobates. Believing we must live our lives to satisfy other's expectations of us and that stuttering jeopardizes our chance of doing so, we feel ill-at-ease much of the time.

At times, we, too, may experience happiness. But our happiness, if tinged with relief that we spoke without stuttering, does not last. Such happiness is *ordinary happiness.* Ordinary happiness arises when we have what we want, and it absconds when we lose or fear we may lose that object of our desire. Most of us, whether we have a stuttering problem or not and whether we realize it or not, put ourselves on the path of seeking ordinary happiness and, consequently, feel let down most of the time. We feel happy when we speak as we wish and unhappy when we do not. We feel elated having a stutter-free phone conversation with technical support staff about our new headphones early in the day and unhappy eating a cheese sandwich for dinner because we were afraid we would stutter phoning in a pizza order. We feel happy making a presentation to our graduate class in economics when we say exactly what we want to say without stuttering and unhappy experiencing rejection after stuttering intensely asking someone we like to join us for dinner. We feel happy getting the unanimous support of our co-workers for undertaking a task we identify as necessary at our weekly staff meeting after making the presentation without stuttering and by saying exactly what we wanted to say and unhappy hours later as we stutter so fiercely we needed to repeat our credit card number several times to be understood making an auto insurance premium payment over the telephone, and so on. And so it goes.

When we seek happiness by not stuttering, we live like a yo-yo. We cycle from up to down and from down to up. We feel happy. Then we feel sad. We feel sad. Then we feel happy. Enduring happiness eludes us when we base our expectation for lasting happiness, at least partly, on stutter-free speech. To do so is like expecting extended bliss from torrid coupling. Sexual desire and the opportunity to express it come and go offering pleasurable anticipation and relief or disappointment and frustration, none of which lasts. Similarly, stutter-free speech also comes and goes as does the happiness we derive from it.

The true happiness we may seek arises as we challenge the belief that our path to true happiness is speaking without stuttering and when we recognize, that as someone with a stuttering problem, we are not alone. Others, too, near and far, feel misunderstood, unappreciated, and apart sometimes whether or not they have a stuttering problem. Thinking of them and doing what we can to comfort and help direct them to a happier life can ignite true happiness in us by increasing our participation with others while diminishing our fear of rejection. Wading or diving into that maelstrom called humanity, we place ourselves on the road to *true happiness,* that state of mind where we can experience fluency or we can experience stuttering in all their many flavors and peace-fully abide, as we recognize and respect our common humanity by living compassionately and with integrity (e.g., Burkeman, 2012; Khyentse, 2012).

9

DOING THE WORK

INTRODUCTION

We all want to change or to help someone change; otherwise, we would not be reading this. What we often do not fully appreciate at the start, though, is that the change we want takes real and hard work often for a prolonged, undetermined period of time for adults. But the process need not be a grim slog. It is what we make it, and that can be a bold and deeply satisfying journey, once we settle down to see clearly what needs to be done and muster the resources we need and possess to make that happen. By addressing our beliefs *and* behavior, not just one or the other, we are apt to succeed and to grow stronger than we ever imagined. That is what I have learned, and that is what I echo in this relatively brief communiqué adapted from *Mind Matters: Setting the Stage for Satisfying Clinical Service. A Personal Essay.* (Silverman, 2009).

WHO DO YOU THINK YOU ARE?

In the West, we seem obsessed with faults. Teens, at an alarming rate, undergo liposuction and breast implantation to correct

91

their self-perceived physical flaws and to resurrect their self-worth. Selling weight loss strategies and accoutrements continue to generate lucrative returns. Self-help books command a significant share of publishers' yearly output. And the shared message of almost all media advertisement is that we can, indeed, should improve our appearance, our fragrance, and our life style. Experiencing such pervasive, relentless, sensory bombardment to convince us to strive toward some crafted notion of social desirability and acceptance, it is not surprising, unless we are a monastic and, possibly, not even then, that we often loose sight of what is right with us. And that is Our Innate Perfection (Chödrön, 2009). Yes. Our Perfection.

Some years ago, according to Pema Chödrön (2005b), Shunryu Suzuki Roshi, Zen Master, mildly amused those gathered to hear him speak at the San Francisco Zen Center by announcing,

You are all perfect, but you could use a little work.

That wry remark reminds us we all are equipped to shine, and we have a personal responsibility to do so, as the beloved gospel song, *"This Little Light of Mine,"* gracefully exhorts. And so it is from a Buddhist perspective, an African-American one, and from Transactional Analysis, which, as a central premise, asserts, "I'm OK. You're OK." (e.g., Harris, 2004), that we realize we do not need to fix ourselves. We need only to grow into the fullness of our marvelous being by cultivating the strengths, talents, and skills we already possess. And I know doing so can help spring release from a vise-like grip of a stuttering problem.

BELIEFS

Deciding whether we are flawed or complete provides a powerful place to start. Considering ourselves flawed, we will be less likely to enthusiastically and patiently commit to the tasks involved to become as we wish and more likely to feel angry and fearful than if we think of ourselves as whole. Don't take my word for it. Experience for yourself effects these beliefs may have on your thoughts, emotions, sensations, and behavior by performing the following two visualizations.

If you are uncomfortable for any reason with the thought of performing them, then, please, do not do so. You might feel like doing so another time, or you might not. That is all right. Trust your feelings.

Visualization: Flawed/Complete

(Hint. You may wish to record the directions then follow them later as you listen to them, or you may prefer to follow them while someone reads them aloud.)

I

Find a quiet place free of external distractions, then sit erect on a chair with your feet firmly on the floor and hands palm down, right hand resting on right thigh, left hand resting on left thigh. Breathe in slowly, then out slowly. Close your eyes or leave them slightly open focusing on a stable image a foot or so away from where you are sitting. Settle.

Now picture yourself flawed in a particular way. Perhaps, you see yourself limping, stuttering, or obese. Visualize yourself that way. See yourself sitting, perhaps, on a park bench. Observe how you look. Note what you think. Experience your emotions. Pay special attention to how you feel, i.e., Do you feel your body? Are there areas that feel tight? loose? heavy? light? hot? cold?

Release that image from your mind.

When you are ready, see yourself flawed as before but now standing, waiting for an elevator. Observe your appear-

93

ance. Note your thoughts. Experience your emotions. Identify the sensations throughout your body.

Release that image from your mind.

Finally, when you are ready, see yourself, flawed as before, walking through a mall. Observe your appearance. Notice your thoughts. Feel your emotions. Identify the sensations throughout your body.

Release that image from your mind.

Sit quietly for a moment.

II

When you are ready, consider yourself complete. Believe you are no better or no worse than anyone else. Now, see yourself sitting on a park bench. Note your appearance, your thoughts, your emotions, the sensations throughout your body.

Release that image from your mind.

See yourself standing, waiting for an elevator. Note your appearance, your thoughts, your emotions, the sensations throughout your body.

Release that image from your mind.

Finally, see yourself walking through a mall. Once again, note your appearance, your thoughts, your emotions, the sensations of your body.

Release that image from your mind.

Draw in a deep breath then slowly release it.

Return to the present.

Perhaps, visualizing yourself as flawed, you had difficulty attending to sensations throughout your body because you were so busy thinking about being accepted. Maybe you did feel your body and noticed that in some areas or throughout it felt constricted, heavy, even cool or cold, quite different from when you visualized yourself as complete. Then you may have noticed areas that felt warm, light, at ease, even spacious. And your thoughts and emotions may have tilted from uncertainty and anxiety toward confidence and enthusiasm when you saw yourself as complete rather than as flawed.

This brief, directed experience may have revealed or confirmed the reality that beliefs about who we think we are generate associated thoughts, behaviors, emotions, and sensations ultimately compatible or antagonistic to desired change.

Consider the history-making 2008 USA presidential campaign. By adopting the galvanizing slogan, "Yes We Can," Barack Obama, with his soaring rhetoric, inspired young voters, who previously had considered themselves politically insignificant, to believe they were powerful. When they enthusiastically and tirelessly put the belief that their voice mattered into action by staffing offices, phoning, canvassing neighborhoods, etc., they helped change the world.

Many of us who have stuttering problems often concentrate on what is wrong with us. Just ask, and we will readily tell you:

We can't say certain sounds and words.

We can't answer the telephone.

We can't make presentations.

We can't tell a joke.

Etc.

But if a therapist surprises us by asking what is right with us, we may become dazed. We may need time to answer. We even may need coaxing. We labor under the belief life for us goes wrong, not right. We are, after all PWS's, People Who Stutter. Separate. Different. Eventually, we may recognize that perceiving ourselves as outsiders constitutes much of our problem. When we begin seeing ourselves as complete, no better nor no worse than anyone else, we can begin to erase this false notion.

BEHAVIOR

When we think stuttering marks us as damaged goods, our response to further stuttering becomes resistance, avoidance, and struggle, reactions which do not end our stuttering problems but grow them. Anger, resentment, regret, bitterness, and, even, cynicism increase. Our stuttering behaviors layer more intricately. And, typically, we talk less. So, I prefer a self-view based on the recognition of our shared humanity. This perception supports greater understanding of and confidence in who we are fundamentally, more space within which to function, and a distinct platform from which to select helpful strategies for change. From personal experience with this orientation (Silverman, 2005; 2003), my preference for deep healing (e.g., Das, 2003; Weil, 1995) involves meditation, specifically a combination of *vipassana*, or mindfulness, practice (e.g., Kabat-Zinn, 2005: Kornfield, 2003), *shenpa* practice (e.g., Chödrön, 2003b; Silverman, 2005), and *tonglen* practice (e.g, Chödrön, 2003b). Mindfulness practice heightens our awareness of our bodily sensations, thoughts, and emotions as they arise. *Shenpa* practice teaches remaining with, rather than resisting, unwanted, unpleasant circumstances. And *tonglen* practice, at the simplest level, allows us to affirm our shared humanity, especially with those feeling embarrassment, shame, and fear wherever we are and whenever we wish. Altogether, they provide coherence and power to our change process because they stem from and reinforce the belief we are complete in our essence.

BEYOND

Even monkeys fall out of trees.

- - - Japanese proverb

Carl Gustav Jung, the pioneering psychoanalyst, when questioned toward the end of his life whether he believed in God responded smiling somewhat enigmatically, *"I know. I do not need to believe. I know."* (Whitney, 1986). And so it is with us. When we change our behavior to coincide with the belief we are complete, we no longer need to believe that is our identity. *We know.*

Does that mean we never relapse? Of course not. We do. The most basic trigger for stuttering, beyond linguistic and social uncertainty, seems to remain unknown, but our habitual avoidance response to it, made strong after years of practice, may persist for some time. But, continuing with *vipassana, shenpa,* and *tonglen* practices, we can say to ourselves following a moment of stuttering, "NO BIG DEAL!" just as we can after engaging in a brilliantly successful conversation or making a well-received presentation. We are, after all, beyond all that. We are perfect.

I would like to express my appreciation to Cindy Spillers for reading and commenting on a preconference version of this manuscript.

ഔ COMMENTARY ഔ

TRUE VIEW

Changing how we speak can take considerable time. That is the inescapable reality no one wants to think about too much when the bug to change strikes. We are eager to begin. We research methods, products, and specialists. We gauge which may best mesh with our nature and expectations. And we assess what we can afford financially and time-wise. On the surface, we seem to be using our time well by minimizing the possibility we will engage in unproductive, distracting, and counterproductive activities that may drain us physically, emotionally, financially, and, perhaps, psychically. But we may be wasting our time unless we first reflect on whether or not we believe we *deserve* to speak with greater ease. If we do not believe we deserve to live more happily than we are, we will not succeed, no matter how much time, money, and effort we spend on whatever method or methods and personnel we may select to learn to help us speak with greater ease. If we want to use our time well, we first will look inward.

Believing ourselves unworthy of desired change differs fundamentally from doubting we can change. Doubting boldly asserts itself. We can feel doubt in our body and through our emotions. We can see doubt reflected in our choices and through our action and inaction. And we can hear doubt embedded in our self-talk. Doubt reflects our uncertainty about doing what we have not done before, or functioning according to our expectations, and, in so doing, doubt can spur us to take its challenge to be different and to do more and to act more skillfully. Doubt can help us broaden our outlook and cultivate new skills. Doubt can open doors to desired change. And doubt dissolves when we do what it proclaims we can not.

Believing ourselves unworthy presents more subtly. Failing repeatedly to do what we seemingly strive for can mask a belief of unworthiness. So, too, can seemingly, otherwise, unaccountable bouts of sadness, lethargy, and despair, which also may be signs of *acedia* defined as spiritual torment (e.g., Norris, 2008) or of *malaise*. Recurring self-deprecatory remarks and self-destructive behavior, including addictions of all kinds, also can reveal a belief of unworthiness. Disbelieving our worthiness to live with greater happiness can slam the door on desired change and can prevent us, at least temporarily, from even seeing the door.

Doing The Work

Believing we are unworthy to be happier than we are arises from adopting the destructive and false view that we are fundamentally flawed, a perception we may have been coerced to accept as was, for a time, the fictional, very young Harry Potter, whose *muggle* caretakers did not want him to know who and what he was to satisfy their needs for self-acceptance and, possibly, to exact the revenge to which they felt entitled because they believed they, as his relatives, should have been born at least as spiritually gifted as he. This falsehood fosters an obsession with fault-finding, a tendency toward harsh judgment of self and others, and a great amount of difficulty acknowledging strengths and talents, personal and otherwise. For instance, caregivers resentful that a child's ability and talents outshines their own may compliment the child on some seemingly insignificant accomplishment, such as neatly arranging the table flatware in a kitchen drawer, while belittling or ignoring especially significant ones, such as earning "A's," as did mine to encourage conformity with their world view and circumstance. The cumulative effect of refusing to acknowledge a child's genuine and particular talents can encourage the child to develop a *persona* of anger and sadness that can lead to marginal rejection by classmates, fellow employees, acquaintances, and others that can reflexively induce a chronic sense of personal unworthiness, or contribute to an existing one. When we come to believe we need to suppress aspects of who we are to be accepted because, in our totality, we are inherently flawed, we set the stage for unremitting sadness and anger to become ruling forces in our daily lives.

In such repressive childhood climates, stuttering problems, not stuttering *per se*, may arise from and feed on the twin beliefs that stuttering is bad and that we are bad if we stutter. Our riff on them portrays us as weak, even unprincipled and unredeemable, if we do not stop stuttering. Unless successfully challenged, this misperception can worm its way into our subconscious where, impervious to casual detection, it can imperiously direct our thoughts and behavior, eventually cloaking us in the shame of perceived unworthiness

99

that encourages us to abandon the hope of experiencing jobs, friendships, and relationships we desire. Substituting a true view of ourselves for this false one becomes *the* work for many of us who have lived most of our lives in the West where self-denigration prevails, whether or not we have a stuttering problem.

We can begin by showing ourselves kindness when our inclination is to berate ourselves for having short-changed ourselves in the past or in the present by what we thought or what we did. We can choose instead to compliment ourselves for what we are doing now, embracing the vision, the courage, and the determination to change. We can appreciate ourselves for noticing what we are thinking and doing moment-by-moment, step-by-step and making corrections we believe necessary to proceed without lapsing into a harsh criticism that shrivels rather than enlarges our motivation to move forward. For instance, as we notice ourselves holding our breath as we struggle to stop stuttering, we can simply observe our behavior without crossly denouncing ourselves for lapsing into that counterproductive, habitual, fear-based reaction we have to stuttering. Just noticing what we are doing then calmly substituting a more useful thought or behavior without editorializing helps us more consistently be and do as we wish.

Nothing useful comes from berating ourselves for what we have or have not thought or done. Showing ourselves respect by expecting ourselves to be capable of thinking and doing what serves us well and then doing that is what propels us into a phase of life where we feel worthy to enjoy speaking and communicating with greater ease more consistently and then do so. There will be times, though, when we do not succeed as we wish, since that is a common experience for all. Perhaps, we were not yet skilled enough or obstacles we did not foresee arrived that were too strong for us to surmount. Maybe we will meet, even exceed, that goal sometime. Or maybe that goal will remain unattainable for us. We do not know. But we do know that berating ourselves for not doing what we wish at the time upsets us and can interfere with being more as we wish.

Some say, "Seeing is believing." Others say, "Believing is seeing." Which is true? Does it matter? Evidence from cognitive and neuroscience reveals that belief triggers and is shaped by experience while experience leads to and modifies belief. Belief induces us to do this, not that, and what we do strengthens or weakens belief. Perhaps neither view that we are fundamentally flawed or fundamentally perfect accurately represents who and what we are. We may never know while we live on Earth. But we do know that belief orchestrates behavior and that no belief has a more far-reaching effect on our ability to change the way we speak and communicate than what we believe about our inherent worthiness for greater happiness. Believing ourselves unworthy, we will not achieve it; believing we are, ignites and sustains the process. We do not believe something is true because we see it; we see that something is true because we believe it is. For our own sake and for the sake of others, we need to see clearly who and what we are.

10

MY STUTTERING IS ME

INTRODUCTION

Is she kidding? She's her stuttering! How pathetic.

If I read *"My Stuttering is Me"* as the title of someone's paper, those thoughts or ones similar to them might immediately come to mind, since I function somewhat judgmentally. But you may be curious instead, simply wondering what I might mean. So, let me assuage your interest by confiding that I do mean what I say in the title but possibly not in the way you initially may think. I believe it is possible to define ourselves much too narrowly to encourage our desired growth. And I believe we can take the action needed to speak more as we wish when we first acknowledge what it is that we do to interfere with that desire. Let me explain.

Imagine

I have intermittently grappled with the question, *"Who Am I?"* not necessarily because I am a slow learner, although I may be, but because, as you know, this is a vast subject to comprehend. And not to be outdone in time spent within the category of ongoing contemplation has been my twin pre-occupation with finding the appropriate path through life. As you may suspect, all this existential, mental adventuring has been heavily colored by my feelings about speaking, as the following story suggests.

Imagine yourself, if you will, sitting quietly in a straight back chair with your eyes almost closed and asking, *"Who am I?"* You are addressing whatever or whomever you believe may be able to satisfactorily answer your question. You wait almost patiently for a time, then, just as you are about to end the seemingly futile exercise and go about your mundane activities, you hear the words spoken faintly by a non-descript voice in your head say, *"A Stutterer."* With a jolt arising from both disbelief and displeasure, you leap from your chair. Angrily, you refuse to accept this is all you are. You are an accountant, a parent, a deacon in your church. You garden, practice photography, paint in water-color and oil. Neighbors come to you for advice. You advocate for the poor and displaced. You even have considered running for public office.

"A Stutterer? That's all I am to You?" you shout in outrage, posturing yourself to duke it out if need be. *"A Stutterer?"*

"No," retorts the same silent voice you heard before, *"But that is Who You Think You Are."*

I present this apocryphal story to reinforce two fairly widely-held truths:

1. We retain, perhaps in our subconscious, a deep personal conception of who we are that is greater than we ordinarily acknowledge. That is why being seen as less than we know we are leads us to respond with some degree of anger or despair. And

2. No one else, not even the wisest among us, can tell us who we are. That task is ours alone to discover. That is

true whether we have or have had a stuttering problem or not, if our goal is to be happy and to live with ease (Hanh, 2005).

That some of us have stuttering problems and some of us never have or will in no way separates us fundamentally from one another. We all desire to be happy and live in peace. Whether we have a stuttering problem, play the piano, struggle to quit smoking or an addiction of some other kind, enjoy animal companionship, dislike physical exercise, cook with zest, fear change, orate with power and finesse, or exhibit other challenges, accomplishments, and tendencies, we are similar at our core. Taking responsibility for our beliefs and actions leads to increasingly recognizing this is so.

Now, picture yourself opening a set of Russian nesting dolls. The outermost doll painted to represent a smiling peasant woman clad in a brightly colored, patterned dress covered with a gaily ornate blouse-like apron wears a boldly patterned *babushka,* or head scarf. Twisting the head and upper torso apart from the rest of it reveals another similarly painted doll contained inside. Opening that one, you find another painted doll inside and so-on and so-on until you find a wee figure shaped like those which had surrounded it but lacking the surface detail that characterized them. This tiny object that you can grasp between your thumb and forefinger and painted red is far less revealing of what it may be than, say, an embryo.

As we work to discard the often colorful, false, and limiting notions of who we are that family, religion, culture, society, and our genera-tion encourages us to adopt to be accepted (e.g., Berne, 1996), we increasingly resemble the nondescript doll nestled deep within the multiple painted caricatures. From that newness of being, we can begin to make informed choices and to acquire the experience and develop the skills to be as we wish. And, as we do so, we become increasingly refreshed, capable, and confident (e.g., Matthew, 16:25), as did Neo, the lead character in the movie, *The Matrix.*

ACT

Uncovering, then cultivating, our genuine self may take most of our adult life (Jung, 1986). Psychoanalyst Dr. Carl Jung recognized the process of applying insight to uncover and destabilize layers of conditioned thought and behavior we accumulate by adulthood as essentially an educational one (e.g., von Franz, 1964). The founder of Transactional Analysis, Eric Berne (e.g., 1996), also committed to helping others discover and live as their authentic selves, emphasized action over insight. He told patients to " . . . *change first, and we'll talk about why you behaved as you did later.*" (Woollams & Brown, 1979).

Those of us with stuttering problems often favor the approach suggested by Dr. Berne. We want to speak with greater ease as soon as possible. Tired of living as we have, dominated by anxious thoughts that coerce us to live as risk-free as possible, a stance that increasingly constricts our lives, we become eager for quick results. Long term commitment to personal growth, on the other hand, even if it provides the durable change we seek without exposing ourselves to the same degree of risk of being exploited, may seem unnecessary when all we want is to stop stuttering *now*. But, as usual, following the middle road brings the greatest satisfaction (Martin, 2005). By simultaneously addressing our speech needs along with our desire for fundamental change, we develop clearer views of ourselves, others, and the world and learn how best to act on them, and we speak and experience life more as we wish (e.g., Silverman, 2010; 2009b).

BE

Medical intuitive Caroline Myss (2009) and psychotherapist Thomas Moore (2010), among others, advise that the more clearly we see ourselves, the more deeply we understand our problems can not name us. We are so much more than our stuttering. Honoring that reality, we can choose to live expansively with curiosity and courage, or not. I, personally, have found the ancient practice of mindfulness, particularly the little-known one labeled *shenpa* (e.g., Chödrön, 2006; Silverman, 2005), especially helpful for learning to relate skillfully to my stuttering. *Shenpa* practice provides convincing motivation and useful skills to comfortably face, rather than resist, all aspects of stuttering problems including talking with certain people and in specific situations as well as various stuttering form-types themselves. In fact, a contemporary definition of mindfulness as ". . . the open heart" (Winston, 2010, p. 31) well describes what I am learning after more than 17 years of mindfulness practice. For when we come to open our heart to our triumphs and tragedies alike, we become fearless. We no longer fear, and we begin to comprehend who we are.

ME

Who am I? Not my stuttering. That is certain. Like you, I am someone with traits, sensibilities, and a bevy of characteristics. Sometimes I stutter, and sometimes I trip, yet I keep going. As the poet Ranier Maria Rilke advised,

Let everything happen to you

Beauty and terror

Just keep going

No feeling is final.

In that way, I have learned that stuttering is something I can manage as I wish. It is no more me than my tendencies to overeat and limp. *Who am I?* Someone grateful to be exploring the great vastness of what I call Me.

POSTSCRIPT

I have chosen to address this critical topic recognizing who we believe we are fashions how we live. Take stuttering, for example; when we see ourselves as capable and wise, we come to expect that we can learn to make helpful decisions and take useful actions to speak with increasing ease. If we see ourselves differently, perhaps as fundamentally flawed, we despair that that is possible. We may easily draw down into a proverbial shell separating ourselves from others and our own true nature to live in fear rather than fully and with joy. The choice is ours. Fundamentally, we know this is true, but, occasionally, we require reminders this is so. So, the essential message here is that taking the time to know who we are at the deepest level of our being is the most practical gift we can give ourselves.

ᔤ COMMENTARY ᔤ

BEING AS WE ARE

Being who we are moment-by-moment puts us on course to experience the change we desire more consistently. But when we feel stressed seeking acceptable employment, relating constructively to family members, speaking with management at work, locating materials and skilled technicians to keep our 18-year-old sedan running safely, stretching our household budget to pay increasing utility charges, or in any other circumstance that challenges us to be level-headed, we may consider the suggestion to be who we are naive and unattainable. We question how we can smile convincingly discovering we owe $5,000 in back taxes plus penalties because our accountant made an error with a previous year's tax filing, noticing a row of shingles curling along the peak of our roof, learning our 14-year-old daughter skips mathematics class to write pop songs, and during the myriad additional times life seems to be slapping us hard across the face. What we feel like doing when we feel bitch-slapped by life is to scream, swear, hit, or pull the bedcovers over our head. What we do not feel like doing is smiling. Smiling would require acting skills we neither have nor wish to have.

But smiling when we feel angry, hurt, disappointed, or frightened is not being as we are. *Being who we are involves being as we are in the moment* rather than acting. When we are angry, we acknowledge we are angry, then responsibly resolve our anger. We are do not engage in excessive politeness to push down our anger to be liked, a pretense which distances us emotionally from others and can trigger inappropriate outbursts later. When we are sad, we recognize we are sad, then respond skillfully to our sadness. We do not substitute excessive cheeriness for sorrow and grief to act strong, which walls us off emotionally from others. When we are afraid, we admit we are afraid, then calmly observe our thoughts and bodily sensations to learn how fear expresses itself within us to learn ways of constructively allaying our fear. We do not automatically withdraw or engage in reckless challenges to convince ourselves and others we are tough.

Being who we are we do not stop being as we are to act how we think we should act. For example, the nun playing a nun in the largely improvised and highly acclaimed Canadian film, *Strangers In Good Company* (1990), farts with a flourish as the transparent, ebullient individual she is. She neither muffles nor constrains the gas seeking release to appear inoffensive or lady-like. Her choice to "let it rip" serves as a stark and memorable object lesson for us: Being who we are is being as we are right here, right now, gaseous and all. Being who we are is not acting to convince ourselves and others we are an idealized person who speaks perfectly, never hesitating, never stuttering. Being who we are is not pretending to be a fully realized being.

Being as we are is the first step to being as we wish to be more consistently. Knowing and accepting ourselves as we are we are in the moment, where we have the insight and greatest opportunity to think and act in ways that move us toward our goal of speaking and communicating with greater ease more consistently, positions us to do so. Recognizing we are tensing our abdomen, squeezing the muscles surrounding our eyes, and pressing our lips against our teeth preparing to hold back a stutter, then immediately and dispassionately allowing ourselves to continue doing so creates apparent magic. The mere decision to accept what we are doing in the moment, nothing more and nothing less, releases us from the dynamic of fighting for control of our mind and our body to force them to be and do what *we* want them to be and do. And, almost as soon as we allow our mind-body to be as *it* wishes to be, it becomes more as we wish it to be. Our non-judgmental attention to our thoughts and behavior, any thought and any behavior, neutralizes it, and we almost immediately become more present and calm, capable of being as we believe we need to be. Relinquishing our fear-based desire to control our mind-body to present an idealized image of who and what we are frees it to be as we wish with increasing ease and assurance.

By respecting ourselves as we are, stuttering and all, we are we able to summon the courage, the strength, and the persistence to make the changes we want to make in our beliefs and behaviors to speak and communicate as we wish and to do so more consistently. Just as we are more likely to come to the aid of a friend than an enemy, we are more likely to take time to refresh our beliefs and to practice and hone the skills we need to help us speak more as we wish if we first respect ourselves. Waiting until we function as we desire to relate to ourselves in a friendly, caring, and encouraging manner can sabotage our work to change. After all, why would we do the work for someone we dislike or disrespect.

Cherishing ourselves as we are, stuttering or not stuttering, withdrawn or outgoing, quiet or talkative (e.g., Cain, 2012) provides the spark and momentum to do the work to make the change we want. And, when we do, we do not become someone different from who we are by speaking with greater ease, although we may do some things we have not done and not do some things we have done. We become more at ease and, perhaps, more confident and happy being as we are. We set free the person we have known all along to be who we are.

11

WHAT TO EXPECT FROM MINDFULNESS

INTRODUCTION

When I began practicing mindfulness 15 years ago, I did so somewhat secretly. I believed if those around me knew I was engaging in an activity they would consider exotic they would relate to me as though I had joined "hippy-dom" to "bliss-out" and they would reject me. I thought that because I believed if they knew I was meditating they would think I had rejected them, people who faced life's challenges square-on as they wanted to believe they did. Since I had no desire to withstand such unfound criticism nor to defend the virtues of a practice I was only beginning to experience but for which, based on what I had heard, I had great expectations as a safe method to manage the mounting stress I was experiencing, I did not tell them about my practice. While I doubt those around me today would consider practicing mindfulness quite as "airy-fairy" and off-putting, I believe they, too, would consider a practitioner suspicious, not quite alien but not quite like them either, so I still keep mum with friends, neighbors, and family about my practice, which adds a certain prickliness to my life. Such is the *milieu* in which I reside. Yet, as author Barry Boyce (2011) reports, much of Western society seems to be experiencing a mindfulness revolution. Within the past decade or so, books have been written about mindful parenting, mindful eating, mindful partnerships, mindful leadership, mindful teaching, mindful *yoga*, mindful gardening, being a mindful therapist, and mindful anxiety reduction. Multitudes, it seems, are discovering that this two-thousand, six hundred year-old practice breeds calm and insight even during such stress-provoking times as these of global fiscal uncertainty tied to a growing human population and the over-arching demands that places on our eco-system and national interests.

Now, after 15 years of practice, I am glad I began. And I am glad I am continuing to learn how to use this tool which helps me experience increasing clarity, hopefulness, and calm irrespective of what life brings and to speak and communicate with greater ease under all circumstances. I have shared some of what I have learned through papers presented at previous ISAD Conferences, for instance, "My Personal Experience with Stuttering and Mediation" in 2003, and "*Shenpa*, Stuttering, and Me" in 2005, by applying the deepest lessons mindfulness has to teach: *Be Present. Be Kind* (especially to ourselves).

Because I believe others with stuttering problems also may discover living ever more mindfully helps them speak and communicate more as they wish, I decided to write this paper as encouragement to do so but not as an uncritical "rah-rah" piece. As the fair-minded clinician and researcher I believe I am, I have chosen to communicate an incontrovertible realization from study (e.g., Salzberg, 2011; Chödrön, 2005) and direct experience (e.g., Silverman, 2012; 2005), namely: *Mindfulness is transformative but not easy.* In fact, as Jon Kabat- Zinn (2005, p. 21), the originator of the complementary medical practice of Mindfulness Based Stress Reduction (MBSR), starkly advises, ". . . practicing mindfulness meditation is not for the faint-hearted." The practice, which can be introduced readily (e.g., Salzberg, 2011; Hahn, 2003; 2002), can be frustrating, boring, and uncomfortable, even painful at times to practice yet also inspiring, strengthening, and calming. As with developing a stuttering problem, each person seems to experience a course and time table of learning particular to his or her own circumstance. Yet, there are similarities. We are all human after all.

What outcomes may be expected and what involvement may be required when participating in this essentially self-directed activity constitutes the content of this essay. My hope is that those contemplating whether or not to adopt this time-tested practice, which contemporary neuroscience and cognitive science reveal institutes beneficial changes in brain structure and function (e.g., Begley, 2010/2007; Siegel, 2010), to speak and communicate more as they wish may find this paper useful. It is adapted from *Mindfulness & Stuttering. Using Eastern Strategies to Speak with Greater Ease* (Silverman, 2012).

The title, "What to Expect from Mindfulness," may jar you if you practice mindfulness in any of its many forms (e.g., Kabat-Zinn, 2005) and have heard or read that holding expectations can hinder, even derail, the process. But, if you reflect for a moment, you may recall you began practicing because you heard or read that living mindfully leads to greater health, happiness, and ease in life. This apparent contradiction concerning the role expectation plays toward realizing those often reported outcomes offers a fulcrum around which to consider the cost-benefit ratio of applying mindfulness to stuttering problems, and I will use it as such.

MINDFULNESS

For those relatively new to the concept and even for those quite familiar with it, it is helpful to consider or re-consider what mindfulness is and what it is not. Mindfulness is not a prize for sticking with a plan of action the way tapping into an underground stream may be considered a reward for weeks of hard drilling for water in an arid landscape. Mindfulness is like the drill bit. It is a tool we can use to find inside what many of us desire: Calm and clarity, along with greater ease and happiness. But, unlike other tools, we can not purchase, lend, or borrow mindfulness. Nor can we fabricate it. What we can do is cultivate it. And we can do that through correct instruction combined with courage, patience, and persistence in the application of it (e.g., Salzberg, 2011; Kornfield, 1996). Many cultivate mindfulness through practicing *shamatha-vipassana* meditation (Piver, 2008), as I do (Silverman, 2003; 2005).

EXPECTED OUTCOMES

I began meditating to relieve mounting stress associated with marriage, child rearing, and career building in the early '70's. The thought that meditating may help me speak and communicate with greater ease did not occur to me then or even in 1996 when I began practicing insight, or mindfulness, meditation following the instruction of Jack Kornfield (1996). I did not even realize that the skills I was learning in practice were to be deliberately and directly transferred to ordinary life (e.g., Boyce, 2010; Loori, 2008; Hahn, 2002), although I had glimmers they could. I began to recognize I did not need to let strong emotion linger by fueling it rehashing stories that gave rise to it; I could, instead, gently return my attention to my breath to be present as I did while meditating. And I began noticing when I was telling myself stories in my head rather than attending to what was going on around and inside me. It was in 2003, as I read Pema Chödrön's (2003) article describing *shenpa*, a Tibetan word that names the urge we experience to escape something unpleasant or something that reminds us of something unpleasant, and how to work with it that I recognized the role mindfulness could play in working effectively with stuttering problems, my own and other peoples' by decreasing negative self-talk, increasing self-mastery, and becoming more open.

Decreasing Negative Self-Talk

We seem to talk to ourselves all the while we are awake (e.g., Salzberg, 2011). Becoming increasingly mindful makes that apparent. For someone with a stuttering problem, worrying about stuttering and regretting having stuttered helps maintain the problem. Yet, because we are so accustomed to stutter-related worry, planning, and regret, we frequently fail to notice we occupy ourselves that way. Becoming ever more mindful of what we are silently telling ourselves throughout the day, as we are when we meditate, reduces the amount and intensity of unpleasantness we may experience related to speaking and gives us more time to actually speak. And, as we do when we meditate, we gently release these often unnecessarily critical thoughts to attend with interest, rather than judgment, to what is going on inside and outside us, which builds our confidence and increases our desire to think and act in ways helpful to ourselves and others.

Increasing Self-Mastery

Our view of who we are and how we need to be can become as distorted as our reflection in a funhouse mirror. Ultimately, we exit the darkened funhouse, which is really not a fun place to be at all, and see ourselves and our stuttering in the light of the sun. We recognize that our stuttering is not a marauder we need to conquer. *Our stuttering is what we do* (Williams, 1957). And it is not who we are (Silverman, 2010). *We may never fully know why we stutter, but we can know how we respond to our stuttering. We can,* through the use of mindfulness, observe what we are thinking and telling ourselves before, during, and after we stutter and gently release these thoughts and associated behaviors without getting caught up in them or in blame. *We can,* using mindfulness, feel the energy of our emotions and let them dissipate by refusing to entertain ourselves with stories that intensify and prolong them. *We can*, using mindfulness, carefully observe how we breathe to be present with each in-breath and each out-breath. And, using mindfulness, *we can* notice signs of excess tension in our lips, tongue, jaw, chest, and elsewhere and, with gentle awareness, allow it to release. We do not need to master our stuttering to speak with greater ease. We need to master ourselves. We begin this noble task by first becoming aware of what we are thinking, experiencing, and doing.

Becoming More Open

> *I live my life in widening circles*
> *that reach out across the world.*

> - - - *Rilke's Book of Hours* (Barrows & Macy, p. 45)

As we use mindfulness to become more accustomed to recognizing our thoughts, being with our emotions, noticing our bodily sensations, and monitoring our actions as they arise and more skillful relating to them, we become more participatory (e.g., Hopkins, 2008). Our increasing self-mastery brings greater confidence with the desire to live life more fully. We are more willing to speak-up at home, with acquaintances, with strangers, and even with those we consider difficult. Similarly, we become more willing to speak in diverse settings. We even feel more kindly toward others, having begun to relate more kindly to ourselves. In short, we recognize our undeniable kinship with others and cease to feel separate. Knowing we are not alone, we begin to heal.

EXPECTED EFFORT

If you want to get to the castle, you got to swim the moat.

> - - - "Richard from Texas," (Salt & Murphy, 2010)

What Richard from Texas was telling Liz in the movie *Eat Pray Love* was that she needed to learn to live in the moment if she wanted to realize her desire of having peace. In the next scene, Liz heeds his advice by sitting to meditate. As she settles in, she notes it is 1:59 pm. We see her looking about, scratching her wrist, gazing at the ceiling fan, and noting an insect landing on her neck. We hear her silently wondering where she might live, happily considering building a meditation room, harshly reminding herself to clear her mind, then ruefully asking, "Why is this so hard?" before comparing her distracted efforts to mediate to a seemingly focused individual sitting nearby. Then we see her notice the clock registering 2:00 p.m., and we witness the look of abject horror on her face as she silently declaims, "Oh, my God, kill me!" before darting for the door. One minute meditating temporarily induced furious self-recrimination, a sense of personal defeat, and the social skills of a harridan as she encounters Richard on her flight from the meditation room. Several weeks later, we observe a more focused Liz seated calmly in meditation. With determination, consistency of effort, and skilled guidance, she is more assuredly meditating.

Similar high's and low's await us, too, if we take up the practice. And, if we do, we eventually find ourselves applying to our stuttering problem, *all aspects of it*, the mindfulness skills we learn to quiet our mind and focus our attention and to greet and remain with difficult and with pleasant emotions and bodily sensations as they arise and as they fade. And we live and communicate with increasing ease.

ഇ COMMENTARY ഇ

IMPERMANENCE

There is, perhaps, no more disturbing aspect of stuttering for those of us with stuttering problems than its unpredictability. We never know with certainty when and where we may stutter. We only are certain we will. This uncertainty not only baffles us, as it does Jason, the 10 year-old lead character in *Jason's Secret* (Silverman, 2001), leading us to speculate endlessly and, often, unproductively about why this is true, but it can encourage us to react to this worrisome reality by being hyper-vigilant, an outlook and practice that can lead to living small and cramped lives that drain our energy. We lack ease. Our life becomes one of struggle and the anticipation of struggle.

This *uber* watchfulness encapsulates us within a cloud of worry and doubt that obscures the fullness of the moment, reducing the possibility we will make and execute timely, skillful decisions to speak, communicate, and live more as we wish. Fretting about where we may stutter next, whether we will stutter with this person or that person, during this form of exchange or that one, and so on, we, ironically, stutter more rather than less while jeopardizing our well-being and limiting our opportunity to experience joy by raising our over-all stress level. As Mark Twain, author and humorist and someone unknown to having had a stuttering problem, facetiously remarked, "My life has been filled with terrible misfortune, most of which never happened." But he did not have to live anticipating struggle, as he apparently did, and neither do we. The practice of mindfulness can help those of us with stuttering problem and those of us without such experience free ourselves from the tyranny of fear. By attending to what we are thinking, what emotions we are feeling, what sensations we are feeling in our body, and what we are doing while simultaneously focusing on what is going on around us, we are more likely to live more as we wish than if we are living apprehensively, only dimly aware of the possibilities within our inner and outer circumstances for relief and succor.

As we relate ever more skillfully to the pushes and pulls of the moment during mindfulness meditation, we increase the likelihood we will do so at other times, even when we are stuttering, or believe we may. For instance, if we are attending non-judgmentally to our bodily sensations, especially those related to breathing and speaking, we are likely to breathe and to use our tongue, lips, jaw, and soft palate in ways that support the forward flow of speech and to do so more consistently than if we are fretting about being refused a date with a person we desire, the job we want, the rental unit we like, the car loan we seek, and so on should we stutter. By worrying about what may be rather than attending to what is, we forego the opportunity we have in the moment, *and only in the moment*, to act in our best interest.

Practicing mindfulness helps us recognize and relate skillfully to the transient nature of all forms and experience, a reality which can deeply disturb each and every one of us. Recognizing the possibility that we, who, and what we care about, such as our lives and family, health, home, friends, employment, and environment can be present one moment and gone the next can be overwhelming. We can panic when we are threatened by the loss of what we cherish, including fluency. And we can become undone and consider giving up when we momentarily relapse by reverting to established patterns of thought and behavior associated with stuttering and the likelihood of stuttering as we learn to speak with greater ease by telling ourselves the falsehood we have lost forever the possibility of speaking as we wish.

Nationally, culturally, locally, and personally we create and carry-out strategies to follow paths that minimize uncertainty and risk. We establish and defend our boundaries, and we establish and maintain systems for defending them even when those strategies may not always be in our best interest, currently or later on. Those of us with stuttering problems do whatever we believe we can to speak without stuttering to eliminate or reduce the possibility of rejection and the negative social and economic fall-out we believe stuttering may bring. We scheme to avoid exposure as someone who has a stuttering problem by devising excuses for refusing to speak when and where we believe we may stutter and we refrain from saying what we really believe, even if that means uttering a blatant lie that could undo us.

The awareness we might stutter at any time arises when we are children living within the context of a family, culture or society that believes difference may be debilitating. We may translate this awareness into the fear that we may be rejected by anyone at any-time and not "fit in," then live that belief. If that is what we do, we owe it to ourselves to thoughtfully scrutinize that fear. Doing so, we may discover that our family, culture, and society no longer believe in such strict conformity, preferring, instead, that each of us find and live the path that helps us enjoy being a contributing member of the group. And, even if members of these groups continue to prefer conformity to their ideals to the expression of individuality, we may discover that we ourselves now posses the stamina and the means to live as we wish without resorting to the draining and calamitous experience living a lie can exact as revealed by the life experience of the tragic, fictional character Albert Nobbs portrayed by Glenn Close in the film of the same name. Film critic, David Edelstein (2012) describes Nobbs, a female passing as a male for economic advantage in 19th century Ireland, as the ". . . personification of fear –– the fear of being seen through, seen for what she is."

We know we can expect to stutter sometimes and not others and more conspicuously sometimes than others, and we wish that were not so. We prefer to never stutter. And because that is our wish, we somehow believe we should be able to realize it. But that is delusional thinking (e.g., Didion, 2007), out of sync with consensus experience. So, if we act to banish stuttering from our life, we can feel a personal and profound sense of failure when the seemingly inevitable occurs and we stutter yet again and, perhaps, fiercely, or we resume fretting about stuttering to the extent that our fear of stuttering again governs our day-to-day lives. But, if we accept the transitory nature of stuttering and the impermanence of fluency as inevitable and if we use that reality as an opportunity to develop greater understanding of ourselves and our stuttering, nothing more and nothing less, without embellishing the temporary reappearance of stuttering and the temporary loss of fluency with self-deprecatory comments ascribing failure and weakness to our character, we can live happier lives and, quite possibly, stutter less often, less fiercely, and, certainly, with less remorse.

That is what I have come to experience through the practice of mindfulness (Silverman, 2012a). By living fully and with kindness toward ourselves, relying on mindfulness to know what actually is as distinguished from the stories we tell ourselves about what is going on inside and outside of ourselves, we can live with increasing ease in the face of the transitory nature of all that we experience, including our stuttering.

12
WHY SEEK THERAPY

Many of us hold assumptions, of which we may be only dimly aware, that, nonetheless, drive our decision to enroll in therapy, or not. These beliefs rather than leading us to experience greater satisfaction can waylay the possibility. Exposing them to subject them to rectification so they become helpful or discarding them if that seems impossible helps us speak and live more as we wish.

INTRODUCTION

Seeking Changes/Seeking Therapy

It is a given: When we are sad, fearful, and angry, we are likely to be more reactionary than deliberate. So, in our 20's, 30's, and 40's, when we feel threatened by potential unemployment, resentful for being under-employed, unfulfilled in personal relationships, or uninspired by what we consider the everyday *blah-ness* of our life, we may reflexively sign on for a stint of speech therapy to shake ourselves out of the doldrums, so accustomed are we to believing or, perhaps, hoping, that, by changing the way we speak, we will live more as we wish. For instance, a 30-something man who worked as a commercial airline pilot recently contacted me. He feared present and future economic crises could trigger staff cutbacks where he worked and, if so, he might be singled out for dismissal if he continued to stutter making in-flight announcements. After years of successful employment and knowing how to respond to discrimination in the workplace, he now believed he needed to stop stuttering to secure his job. He may have been correct. But the fear was insufficient cause, of itself, to enroll in speech therapy, although, by motivating him to contact a speech pathologist to relate his concern, he did experience some relief.

A parallel version of this belief inspires some of us to work as speech pathologists. Many, and I among them, were delighted to learn we could earn a living helping others speak with greater ease and clarity. Yet, because those of us who have stuttering problems and those of us who are clinicians often approach this common belief with differing sets of expectations about our roles and responsibilities when working with one another, we can come to loggerheads. But that need not stop us. We can work our way through these impasses using unflinching self-reflection and negotiation (e.g., Silverman, 2012c; 2009b; 2001).

BEING HONEST WITH OURSELVES

Self-reflection jump-starts the possibility of desired change. This quiet process helps those of us who are clinicians know our true motivation for engaging with clients, which may not be what we readily think (e.g., Silverman, 2011b; 2009b; 2008), and it helps those of us with stuttering problems identify our true motivation for engaging with clinicians, which, also, may differ from what we think (e.g., Hahn, 2006). Motivations have deep roots (e.g., Berne, 1996) and, like the roots of living things, such as trees and shrubs, we usually need to dig beneath the surface to expose them. And so it may be with our true motivation for seeking therapy.

Motivation fashions behavior (e.g., Boorstein, 2012; Mipham, 2012). Our true intent for participating in therapy may be to change how we think and act or it may be to stay the same. So, if we intend to speak with greater ease and confidence more consistently, we will find ways to do that, which may mean choosing to actively participate in speech therapy as well as other personal growth activities to learn tools for change and ways to safely incorporate change into our lives. And, if our motivation is to continue as we are, we will do that, which may involve enrolling in speech therapy only to pay lip service to changing. We may do so deliberately or without conscious awareness. Let me explain.

A Conscious Intent Not to Change

Here are two examples:

1. As adults, we may enroll but not actively participate to diffuse mounting pressure from family or others to "do something" about our stuttering, which we neither want to do nor believe we can. We may arrive late, cancel sessions, or fail to follow through with assignments. And we continue the charade until the therapist discharges us for not assuming our responsibilities or until we quit because we are tired of wasting our time and money pretending to do something we do not want to do.

   We tell family and others that we tried but could not change. We express our disappointment with the therapist who we say failed to incorporate our wishes regarding content, show compassion for our pain and suffering, demonstrate a workable knowledge of stuttering and stuttering problems, or meet our expectations in other ways (e.g., Silverman and Zimmer, 1982). Our rueful confessions usually stifle further suggestions that we change, at least for the present, providing us with the relief we sought by enrolling (e.g., Myss, 1998).

2. Minors in the United States sometimes behave this way. Enrolled by parents and therapists despite their subtle or unmistakable protestations, which do not require x-ray vision to detect, they may resist active involvement to be discharged.

    They may believe classmates will ridicule them for needing help talking as did Jason, the 10-year-old lead character in *Jason's Secret* (Silverman, 2001), who believed going to therapy would mark him a "Freak." Some have other reasons, such as not wanting to miss a favorite class or perform specific therapy tasks. But, if they do not want to attend, they will not participate sufficiently to change as caregivers, professionals, and, even, they may wish.

A Subconscious Intent Not to Change

Reacting to the pervasive anger and sadness we may hold for failing to have overcome our stuttering problem despite attending therapy for years, we now may gravitate toward therapy primarily as avengers. *Our goal*: To expose the inability of therapy and therapists to help. *Our tactic*: To deny the therapist the opportunity to help by refusing to respond to directions and suggestions. *Our payoff*: To draw blood, not to change. Yet, we may be only dimly aware of this. We even may be telling ourselves and others we are re-entering therapy to change.

Human psychology, Eastern (e.g., Kornfield, 2009; Hahn, 2006; Reynolds, 1980; 1976) and Western (e.g., Berne, 1996; Steiner, 1994; Whitney, 1986), offers insight into this stark, subconscious tendency to hurt others to lessen our own pain. Successfully doing so requires a willing partner. Eric Berne (1996), founder of Transactional Analysis, describes this unwholesome partnership in *The Rescue*

Triangle, a psychological game played to evade personal change (e.g., Myss, 1998). The game begins with the players relating amicably, at least superficially, and ends in a seemingly surprising twist with inevitable blood-letting. In a 2001 ISAD Conference paper, "Consumer Alert: Gender and Stuttering Research," I summarized the roles, activities, and payoffs for the players. Here is a recap:

The Rescue Triangle is an interpersonal game for two with three interchangeable roles, Victim, Rescuer, and Persecutor. To start, one player assumes the role of Rescuer, the other, Victim. The Rescuer (therapist) believes his or her task is to manage others' lives and only feels okay when doing so. The Victim (client) seeks help but does not want to be told what to do or how to be. A complementary pair, neither is consciously aware of their own or the other's basic motivation.

Their interactions become increasingly strained as Victim refuses to engage with either the therapist or the process and as Rescuer, fearful of not helping, focuses increasing anger on Victim until, in a stunning turn-around prompted by disappointment, fear, anger, or superiority, one switches roles to become Persecutor. Victim as Persecutor attempts to induce feelings of shame and/or failure in Rescuer by implying Rescuer is too unknowledgeable or unskilled to help him or her, while Rescuer turned Persecutor attempts to inflame feelings of anger and hurt in Victim by implying that he or she can not change.

If the surprised Rescuer succumbs to feelings of anger and hurt for being played this way, he or she becomes Victim; if the astonished Victim experiences anger and hurt for feeling dumped by someone considered inferior, he or she becomes a more entrenched Victim.

The game ends with the original Victim feeling more powerful or more hopeless and with the original Rescuer doubting his or her self-worth for failing to help a client and, possibly, believing adults with stuttering problems cannot be helped. In each scenario, the players feel satisfaction from verifying their initial, subconscious beliefs about themselves and the other.

That sense of being right perpetuates their *status quo,* which brings temporary relief from anxiety but not change.

Playing *The Rescue Triangle* can calcify our stuttering problem or force our development as clinicians into *rigor mortis* (Silverman, 2009b). But we can learn something helpful from anything or anyone at anytime. And what we can learn from playing *The Rescue Triangle* is that trying to subjugate others, even for the loftiest notion, encourages rebellion, insurrection, mayhem, and, ultimately, stagnation. What do we do instead? We take charge. . . of ourselves.

TAKING CHARGE

Some of us may have realized when we were young that we needed to care for ourselves and that that was our primary job in life. We somehow knew we needed to make wise choices and to thoughtfully and skillfully act on them. But, when we were young, we frequently were stifled when we tried. We may have been cared for by people who preferred subordination to our emerging independence and may have tagged us as rebellious and needing a short leash or worse if we acted according to our wishes.

Obedience, rather than collaboration, also may have been our experience in therapy. We, as was Jason, the 10 year-old lead character in *Jason's Secret* (Silverman, 2001), may have been enrolled in speech therapy despite expressing we did not wish to attend. And therapists may have structured the entire experience, from scheduling meeting times and dates to selection of goals and activities, without consulting us. But therapy then does not have to be therapy now.

We need to consider carefully whether and how decisions we made about speech therapy as children and teens may be affecting how we think about speech therapy now. So we use the quintessential tool of self-reflection to clarify what we think and need. Then we identify those who may congenially meet our desire to work as partners and assess honestly our willingness to participate. We are learning that no matter what method we may choose to be as we wish, we will not change unless we change (e.g., Kongtrül, 2006; Silverman, 2009a). Paraphrasing an observation offered by mindfulness meditation teacher Dzigar Kongtrül (2006), *Not even 1,000 speech pathologists can make us change if that is not our wish.*

Children no more, with voices often unheeded, we now choose moment-to-moment what we will and will not do for ourselves. We consider all possibilities, including non-therapy practices, such as mindfulness (e.g., Silverman, 2012; 2011a; Salzberg, 2011) to speak and live as we wish.

MOVING ON

Time to go.

Expert in human consciousness and *New York Times* bestselling author Caroline Myss advises that " . . . the best way to experience a happy tomorrow is by leaving a sad past far behind . . ." (Myss, 1998). Childhood is over. We are no longer teens. Clinging to memories, to feelings about them, and patterns of behavior we adopted then will stymie our wish to change.

We learn to live more skillfully and happily. We do not repress: We recognize. We resolve. We integrate (e.g., Silverman, 2010; von Franz, 1964). We ask ourselves, "Where do I want to go?" (Boorstein, 2012). Then we climb aboard the *Me-Train* and move away and beyond, with or without therapy.

ஒ COMMENTARY ஒ

GROWING UP

Some are grown up at 10, 11, or 12. I took longer. . .

Dr. Carl G. Jung, psychiatrist and pioneering psychoanalyst, who advanced theories of personality and of growth and development, such as *introversion - extroversion,* our personal and collective *shadow, the collective unconscious,* and *the individuation process,* reached the conclusion, after years of analyzing patients' psyches, that we do not overcome our problems. We outgrow them. We grow up (Whitney, 1986). Growing up is what Tibetan Buddhist meditation teacher Chöygam Trungpa Rinpoche also considered the fruit, or realization, of a fully developed human life. Others, too, have come to this understanding, for instance human consciousness student and *New York Times* bestselling author Caroline Myss (1977), psychiatrist and founder of transactional analysis Eric Berne (1996), and editor and author Rachel Neumann (2012). These and other confirmed and dedicated observers consider many of the problems we experience as adults evidence of our need for education rather than signs, *per se*, we need to enroll in lengthy and costly programs of therapy. We can, they suggest, find solutions to many of our personal dilemmas by learning about the spiritual maturation of adults (e.g., Arriens, 2008; von Franz, 1964), practicing self-reflection, and committing to living new or revised personal beliefs rather than just thinking or talking about them. And, if we may occasionally seek the counsel of professionals we consider wise and skilled, these counselors, therapists, and teachers usually remind us that the choices we make about how we live are always ours alone. We have the last word.

This became my experience beginning the day I became 21 and nothing seemed different. Not that I expected celebratory fireworks to pound and puncture the sky at 10:57 the morning of October 12, 1963, when my legal designation changed from non-adult to adult to proclaim that henceforth and forevermore I was certifiably skilled at living sensibly and well. I knew better. But I did expect that, magically, as a gift from the cosmos for reaching that milestone and supposed reconstitution of my identifiable being, I would experience some newness of thought, some twinge of emergent maturity greet me like a lovely and fragrant *lei* of welcome to that state of being where I would evermore decide with ease and assurance what to do and when and how to do it. But that did not happen then or, even, shortly thereafter. Only after trekking for decades forward, backward, sideways, up, down and often painfully and alone through dimly lit passages, along barely recognizable pathways, and across flimsy, swaying bridges suspended over deep, spiky gorges did I become a grown-up, at least in my eyes. Perhaps, I am what an aunt relentlessly critical of me sarcastically proclaimed, " . . . a late bloomer." But I have come to learn that every flower blooms when the causes and conditions required for it to do so combine.

I spent much of my 20's, 30's, and early 40's wanting to know what being grown up looked and felt like. Perhaps, I was deeply unimpressed with and unwilling to settle for a life that resembled the lives of the adults I knew that seemed unhappily repetitive and restrained. Somehow I knew life could be lived more joyfully and more fully as, apparently, did the essayist and wit Fran Lebowitz (Scorsese, 2011), who, as a child, believed women, exemplified by her mother, enjoyed glamorous breakfasts of coffee, toast, and cigarettes, a custom she herself later adopted to signify, at least to herself, that she was grown up or, perhaps, to evade what she considered the pedestrian lifestyle represented by her father whose breakfast consisted of oatmeal and eggs. Or, maybe, I was unreasonably critical of those reactive adults who populated my childhood and teen years because I was delusional and harbored expectations of personal attainment neither realistic nor desired. So, without guidance other than from images thrown up by the media in one form or another and the examples of those I knew, I set out *a la* Elizabeth Gilbert (e.g., 2007) on a so-called truth-finding journey to learn how to live wisely and happily, as I was certain grown-ups could and did.

Smoking, drinking, and getting married, I discovered, did not help, nor did beauty shop appointments, affairs, and winning awards. So I continued looking because I was certain I would not grow up just by growing old. I had witnessed family members and acquaintances in their sixth and seventh decades acting like sad, angry children seizing every opportunity to call out their unhappy childhoods as the cause of their current and prevailing unhappiness. To them, the present generally functioned as a backdrop against which to replay their childhood pain. I did not want to be like them, resentful of others' happiness while fearful to reach out to create my own, waiting, instead, for my luck to change but morose being doubtful it would or could.

Not that I was unsympathetic. I, too, had experienced a dire, bleak childhood filled with enough neglect and abuse to leave me grateful and amazed I had survived. And I, too, bided my time as a child and as a teen waiting for an escape. But I planned for mine. Knowing I wanted to live a life fresh with possibility rather than endure a painful, claustrophobic version of my time at home drove me to climb out of that dismal pit. I aimed for college. I took jobs and saved almost all my earnings. Then I matriculated.

As a freshman of 18, I discovered a major I could complete in the four years of college I could afford that excited me, speech pathology, or speech correction as it was then called, which, at 21, became my entry into and road through the world-at-large. But I still was not living pain-free. Training as a professional gave me rudimentary communication skills sufficient to secure employment, but how to live well as an adult was something I had yet to learn. I was piling pain upon pain attempting to establish myself in personal and work relationships lacking the communication skills to do so that a nurturing childhood could have provided. And that crushing realization that I had not only been robbed of the opportunity to have the loving childhood I believed I and every child deserved but that escaping my hellish childhood did not free me from the pain of rejection KO'd me.

Given the power of childhood experience to shape us, I mindlessly followed the familiar and known model of blaming I had witnessed and despised until my early 40's when I enrolled in a training program for professionals who wanted to use transactional analysis in their work as counselors. That was when I recognized I was creating many of my problems by blaming. I blamed circumstances, family, society, culture, history, religions, other people — caregivers, acquaintances, partners, teachers, co-workers, supervisors, neighbors, and my own child — and God for hurting me rather than helping me live happily. And, perhaps, most damaging I blamed myself, for what I had done or failed to do. I became increasingly stuck in a blame and shame circumstance of my creation impatiently waiting to be rescued by someone I was certain would be wiser and stronger than I who could and would extricate me. When I had waited long enough and sunk as deeply into a dark abyss of my own creation as I could tolerate, I put into practice the realization I had had now and again that my exposure to transactional analysis amplified and fortified: I had the power to change. And I did. I adopted the time-honored strategy of *No Blaming*.

I assumed responsibility for what I thought and did and put that intent into practice by monitoring the linguistic structure of what I said and by attending to what I did so that my words and actions conformed to what I newly chose to believe. I resembled the man described in The Gospels who had been ill for almost four decades and, for quite some time, had been lying on his mat alongside the healing waters of the pool at The Sheep's Gate in Jerusalem hoping someone would put him into that healing water or, at least, prevent others from blocking his way when he tried to make his way into the pool. This was the individual Jesus The Christ instructed, "Rise, take up your pallet, and walk" (John, 5: 8), once the man affirmed he wanted to be healed. Like him I, too, responded to various good advice. I stopped waiting for someone to help me and stopped blaming those who did not seem to help. I relied on myself to do the necessary work. And, I, too, healed.

I learned blaming does not give us what we most want; it gives most of us what we do not — the insinuation we are a victim, perhaps, an eternal one, and that we never may live as we wish. Blaming does not change what we have experienced. Blaming does not replace the unhappy childhood we neither wanted nor believed we deserved with the happy one we wanted and thought we were owed. Blaming does not replace feelings of hurt, fear, and insecurity with confidence and ease when others betray and abandon us. Blaming does not replace feelings of worthlessness and hopelessness with self-respect and dignity if we continue to vilify ourselves for what we did or did not do that brought us regret then and now. And blaming does not absolve us of personal responsibility for how we think and act. For that, we alone are responsible. Once we recognize and embrace that healing truth, we place ourselves squarely on a path of healing or reaffirm the journey.

Sharon Salzberg (2004), teacher of mindfulness, relates a story about an encounter between a spiritual teacher and a student to illustrate that how we choose to think and to act is always our choice. According to Sharon, the student had been describing in detail how horrible his mother had been to him. When he finished his litany of complaint, the great sage queried, "Did you love her?" The student replied, "She never let me." To which the teacher immediately responded, "She could never stop you!" That comment, harsh as it may have seemed to the student at the time, may have helped him see more clearly. Although he may not have drawn on it, he had had the capacity to love his mother. Blaming her for not allowing him to love her, he felt justified in hating her, which may have been what he wished to do. The sage's remark that he had the capacity to act as he wished regardless of her actions toward him unmasked the belief that she was responsible for his current state of unhappiness and that he was blameless for his current circumstance. Likewise, no therapist, no counselor, no parent, no teacher, no friend is responsible for how we think or act or speak — Right here, Right now.

What blaming does is temporarily forestall the anxiety we may experience when we contemplate personal change, specifically the fear we may have that we may not be able to speak and live more as we wish and, paradoxically, the fear that we might, if we recognize that speaking with greater ease positions us to face and shoulder responsibilities in personal and work relationships we neither want nor feel capable of handling well. But the momentary relief we may feel by blaming comes at a high cost. Blaming encapsulates us in shame, regret, anger, sadness, and fear that can create the illusion for us we are separate. And, equally damaging, blaming can stimulate biological reactions within our bodies that trigger depressed mental and physiological functioning which undermines our willingness and ability to benefit from the options present each moment to speak and live more as we wish. That fear-based cocooning can encourage us to sour. When we blame, we pay a high price and, often, a lingering toll to temporarily avoid the occasional, temporary discomfort changing the way we speak and live may bring.

Not long ago, I enlarged my practice of *No Blaming* to include *No Complaining*, which can be a parallel version of blaming. Complaining to relate that life is unfair and that others don't care and can't be trusted, like blaming, stems from the false and perverse belief that others, not we, create our happiness or deny it and broadcasts our belief that change is not for us, that we are stuck like *lifers*, prisoners with no possibility of parole. We are pariahs, and pariahs we will stay. If blaming is shouting, complaining is whining. Yet both provide the same unhealthy rewards. Blaming and complaining garner sympathy, at least from ourselves. And blaming and complaining as we relive past hurts and anticipate future ones distract us from living in the present moment, the place where we have the greatest power and opportunity to live more as we wish.

Soliciting sympathy is how we may choose to relate if blaming and complaining were modeled by our caregivers or if we come to believe we ourselves are incapable of creating and sustaining the emotional energy we need to survive (e.g., Orloff, 2005). Believing sympathy provides the energy we need, we compulsively seek it as any addict searching for a fix. Telling person after person and soliloquizing in our heads about the wrongs individuals and society have inflicted, are inflicting, or may inflict on us by treating us as an "other," we invite and create sympathy to experience a rush of relief from the pain of isolation we, otherwise, would feel. Yet, by ingesting this perverse ambrosia, we weaken ourselves. Even when appearing sympathetic brings financial and other tangible rewards, it ultimately shrinks our lives and increases our pain. For instance, a contestant on a recent reality television show to discover singing talent introduced himself to the judges and the public as someone with a stuttering problem who could sing but who stuttered when he spoke. By demonstrating this seeming curiosity, he generated favorable interest from the judges, the media, and the public for his courage to compete. After reporters quickly discovered reasons to question the truthfulness of his claim that he had a stuttering problem, he was voted off the show, quite possibly as payback from people who felt used by him. Soliciting sympathy for gain quickly became loss for him and increasingly so as he now may have a harder time building a singling career than he, otherwise, might have.

Like him, we, too, may get dumped if others believe we manipulated them by using their need to give to satisfy our need to take (e.g., McGraw, 2013). Whatever our motive may be for seeking sympathy, this form of street currency (e.g., Myss, 1997) distances us from others, strengthening our false and harmful belief we are different and exposing us to rejection by family, friends, co-workers, and acquaintances as they tire of giving time, attention, and support to those who show no genuine interest in helping them satisfy their own wants and needs. The British film, *Cold Comfort Farm*

(1995), showcases a family partially debilitated by a matriarch, who for decades has used her bid for sympathy to cannibalize the emotional and physical resources of her family. This dark comedy provides a view of the havoc Drama Queens and Kings can exact on willing victims and reminds us that true happiness can be experienced when all involved willingly change from co-dependency to self-sufficiency.

Blogs and online and face-to-face support groups for people with stuttering problems can be magnets for sympathy-seeking Drama Queens and Kings. In those environments, where people commonly share personal stories of stutter-related suffering as they go about the task of changing to live more as they wish, Drama Queens and Kings eagerly offer their stories as bait to receive attention and energy, not to seek requests for direction and support, which, if offered, they usually reject saying, "I tried that, and I didn't like it." "I don't have the time for that now." "I don't feel ready to make a change." or some similarly dismissive statement. They play the "Yes. . . But" game described in detail in the book *Games People Play* written by the founder of Transactional Analysis Eric Berne (1966). Their ruse of participating to request information and guidance while actually seeking emotional refueling continues until group members become tapped-out, recognize the deception, or both. Then the Drama Queen or King, who prefers being viewed as pitiful to feeling alone and sad and who is too fearful of personal change to behave differently, migrates to other fields to collect sympathy as mechanically as a bee gathers nectar. When those of us who habitually complain recognize that seeking sympathy as sustenance, like landing on flypaper, can be a trap we can avoid, and that we feel more satisfied and at peace when we relate to ourselves and everyone else in honest, non-manipulative ways, we come to speak with greater ease and do so more consistently.

And those of us who function as enablers by mindlessly offering sympathy to people with stuttering problems who chronically blame and complain may come to recognize that we can be genuinely helpful, as the sage was to the student, when we put another's need to become more skillful ahead of our need to feel good about ourselves. By saying to ourselves in our heads, "He *can* do this." instead of, "I can do that for you." "You don't have to do that; I'll do it for you." "Here, let me do that." or some other such directive, we encourage ourselves to act in a way that feels good to us rather than in a manner genuinely helpful to another and risk creating co-dependency. But we can choose to foster healing relationships instead. Heeding the parable, "Give a hungry man a fish, and you feed him for a day. Teach a hungry man to fish, and you feed him for a lifetime." we can guide people with stuttering problems to discover resources they themselves possess to speak more as they wish. Opening their eyes to their strengths helps them cultivate the self-reliance they need to speak and live with greater ease. And by identifying what we can do for ourselves to feel worthwhile, we live lives of greater use to those around us by freeing them to meet their own needs rather than duping them into living their lives to meet ours.

Those of us who routinely blame and complain may find the pithy and practical advice that H. H. The Dalai Lama gives those who worry too much personally helpful. According to psychologist and meditation teacher Jack Kornfield (2008), The Dalai Lama advises worriers saying, "If the problem has a solution, then there is no need to worry. And, if it has no solution, then there is no need to worry about it anyway." This wise man's message advises us to seek a solution for what impedes us, then enact it And if we cannot find a solution, then to focus on what else we can do to live more as we wish. By concentrating on what we can do to live wisely and well rather than on what has been, is, or may be stopping us from doing so, we live more skillfully and happily and bring greater happiness to those around us. Applying this advice to relating to what angers, annoys, or hurts us helps those of us who frequently blame and complain to live with greater equanimity.

The Dalai Lama's advice echoes that given much earlier by St. Paul, who, when instructing new converts to Christianity on how best to live, said,

> *Whatever is true, whatever is honorable, whatever is just,*
> *whatever is pure, whatever is lovely, whatever is commendable,*
> *if there is any excellence, if there is anything worthy of praise,*
> *think about these things. (Phil. 4:8).*

Centuries later, the poet John Keats who, centuries later, wrote in "*Ode On a Grecian Urn*,"

> *Beauty is truth, truth beauty, — that is all*
> *Ye know on earth, and all ye need to know!*

He, too, may have been telling us to see all that surrounds us, the pleasant and the unpleasant, to recognize and to acknowledge what is true, namely that we have the capacity to see more broadly than we do customarily and that cultivating a more expansive and truer view of circumstances and of ourselves frees us to live and speak with greater ease and satisfaction.

Living *No Blaming* and *No Complaining* helps us live in the moment where we are best able to notice opportunities, face challenges, and to develop and strengthen helpful beliefs and behaviors to live more as we wish. Living *No Blaming* and *No Complaining* we grow stronger and more confident, not all at once, of course, but increasingly as we appreciate each choice as an opportunity to live kindly with respect for ourselves and others, whether we stutter or not and whether we feel respected or not. Living *No Blaming* and *No Complaining* leads to speaking with greater ease. And living *No Blaming* and *No Complaining* leads to growing up.

. . . A word on my behalf: I did the best I could all along. I still do. I have come to realize that we all do the best we can to be happy, no matter what it is that we do, but uuwe rarely feel at peace because what we usually do, such as avoiding stuttering, brings short-lived relief that eventually morphs into increased suffering. But the story does not need to end there. We can learn to relate more skillfully to our thoughts, body sensations, and emotions and to monitor what we do so that we behave in ways to experience an enduring happiness large and steady enough to encompasses our up's and down's while keeping us safely afloat. That is what admired teacher of mindfulness meditation and *New York Times* bestselling author Sharon Salzberg (2012) calls *real happiness*. Structuring my life around that awareness is a distinct sign to me I am growing up, indeed. By assimilating my stuttering rather than distancing myself from it as though it were a distasteful foreign object, I have become more assuredly and fully me, the primary realization of growing up (e.g., von Franz, 1964).

REFERENCES

Agnes, S. (1946). Bibliotherapy for Socially Maladjusted Children. *Catholic Educational Review*, 44, pp. 8-16.

Allione, T., (2008). *Feeding Your Demons. Ancient Wisdom for Solving Inner Conflict.* New York: Little, Brown and Company.

Arriens, A. (2008). *The Second Half of Life. Opening the Eight Gates of Wisdom.* Boulder, Colorado: Sounds True, Inc.

Barrows, A. & Macy, J. (2005). *Rilke's Book of Hours. Love Poems to God.* New York: Penguin Group.

Begley, S. (2010). Forget the cocaine vaccine. Low-tech treatments work better. *Newsweek*, March 14, p. 20.

Begley, S. (2007). *Train Your Mind, Change Your Brain: How a New Science Reveals Our Extraordinary Potential to Transform Ourselves.* New York: Ballantine Books.

Berne, E. (1996). *Games People Play. The Basic Handbook of Transactional Analysis.* New York: Ballantine Books.

Berne, E. (1977). *Intuition and Ego States.* New York: Harper & Row.

Blankenship, J. (1964). "Stuttering" in Normal Speech. *J. Speech Hear Res.,* 7, 95-96.

Boorstein, S. (2012). The Whole of Life as Practice. *Tricycle Magazine, Online Retreat,* April.

Boyce, B. (2011). *The Mindfulness Revolution. Leading Psychologists, Scientists, Artists, and Meditation Teachers on the Power of Mindfulness In Daily Life.* Boston: Shambhala Publications.

Boyce, B., (2010). Why we're taking mindfulness to heart. *Shambhala Sun*, March, p. 11.

Burkeman, O. (2012). *The Antidote: Happiness for People Who Can't Stand Positive Thinking*. London: Faber & Faber.

Byrne, R, Ed. (2006). *The Secret*. New York: Atria Books.

Cain, S. (2012). *Quiet. The Power of Introverts in a World that Can't Stop Talking.*New York: Crown Publishing.

Campbell, J. (1988). *The Power of Myth*. New York: Broadway Books.

Charon, R. (2008). *Narrative Medicine: Honoring the Stories of Illness*. New York: Oxford University Press-USA.

Chess, S. and Thomas, A., (2005). *Temperament in Clinical Practice*. New York: The Guilford Press.

Chödrön, P. (2010). *Taking the Leap: Freeing Ourselves from Old Habits and Fears.* Boston: Shambhala Publications.

Chödrön, P. (2009). *Perfect Just As You Are*. Boston: Shambhala Audio. (CD)

Chödrön, P. (2006). *True Happiness*. Boulder, Colorado: Sounds True. (CD)

Chödrön, P. (2005b). *Practicing Peace in Times of War*. Boston: Shambhala Publications, Inc. (CD)

ChÖdrÖn, P. (2005a). *Getting Unstuck*. Boulder, Colorado: Sounds True. (CD's)

Chödrön, P. (2003b). *Meditation for Difficult Times. Awakening Compassion Through The Practice of Tonglen*. Boulder, Colorado: Sounds True. (CD)

Chödrön, P. (2003a). How we get hooked/How to get unhooked. *Shambhala Sun*, March, pp. 30-35.

REFERENCES

Creswell, J. (2008). *Research Design: Qualitative, Quantitative, and Mixed Methods Approaches*, 3rd Edition. Thousand Oaks, California: Sage Publications, Inc.

Dalai Lama (2001). *An Open Heart.* New York: Little, Brown and Company.

Das, S. (2003). *Letting Go of the Person You Used to Be.* New York: Broadway Books.de Geus, E. (1999). *Sometimes I Just Stutter.* Memphis: The Stuttering Foundation of America.

Didion, J. (2007). *The Year of Magical Thinking.* New York: Vintage Books.

Douglass, E. and Quarrington, B. (1952), The Differentiation of Interiorized and Exteriorized Secondary Stuttering. *J. Speech Hearing Dis.,* 17, (4), pp. 377-385.

Edelstein, D. (2012). Costume Drama. *New York Magazine,* Movies, January 22, 2012.

Estés, C. (1993). *The Gift of Story.* New York: Ballantine Books.

Fraser, J. (1923). *Folklore in the Old Testament.* New York: Macmillan.

Frankl, V., (2006). *Man's Search for Meaning.* Boston: Beacon Press.

Gafni, M. (2004). *The Soul Prints Workshop: Wisdom Teachings from the Kabbalah Illuminating Your Unique Life Purpose.* Boulder: Sounds True, Inc.. (CD's)

Gilbert, E. (2007). *Eat Pray Love. One Woman's Search for Everything Across Italy, India and Indonesia.* New York: Penguin.

Gimian, C., (2008). Beyond Carrot and Stick. *Shambhala Sun,* May, pp. 74-79.

Goleman, D. (1995). *Emotional Intelligence.* New York: Bantam Books.

Goleman, D. (1985). *Vital Lies, Simple Truths.* New York: Simon & Schuster.

Hanh, T. N. (2012). *Fear. Essential Wisdom for Getting Through the Storm.* New York: HarperOne.

Hanh, T. N. (2006). *Mindfulness and Psychotherapy.* Boulder, Colorado: Sounds True, Inc. (CD's)

Hahn, T. N. (2004). *The Ultimate Dimension.* Boulder, Colorado: Sounds True. (CD's)

Hanh, T. N. (2003). *The Present Moment. A Retreat on the Practice of Mindfulness.* Boulder, Colorado: Sounds True, Inc. (CD's)

Hahn, T. N. (2002). *Be Free Where You Are.* Berkeley, California: Parallax Press.

Hanh, T. N. (2000). *The Wisdom of Thich Nhat Hanh.* Pennsylvania: Book-of-the-Month Club, Inc.

Harris, T., (2004). *I'm OK. You're OK.* New York: Harper Paperbacks.

Hellman, L. (1973). *Pentimento.* Boston: Little, Brown, and Company.

Hopkins, J., (2008). *A Truthful Heart. Buddhist Practices for Connecting with Others.* Ithaca, N.Y.: Snow Lion Publications.

Johnson, W. (1956). Stuttering, pp. 216-217. In W. Johnson, *et al.* (Eds.), *Speech*

Handicapped School Children, 2nd Edition. New York: Harper & Brothers.

Jung, C. G. (1986). *Matter of Heart: The Extraordinary Journey of C. G. Jung Into the Soul of Man.* New York: Kino International Corporation. (DVD)

Kabat-Zinn, J. (2005). *Coming to Our Senses. Healing Ourselves and The World Through Mindfulness.* New York: Hyperion

REFERENCES

Kabat-Zinn, J. (1990). *Full Catastrophe Living*. New York: Delacorte Press.

Kabat-Zinn, J. and Davidson, R., Eds. (2012). *The Mind's Own Physician: A Scientific Dialogue with The Dalai Lama on the Healing Power of*

Meditation. Oakland, California: New Harbinger Publications.

Khyentse, J. (2012). Not for Happiness. *Shambhala Sun*, Vol. 21 (3), pp. 35-39.

Klinenberg, E. (2012). *Going Solo. The Extraordinary Rise and Surprising Appeal of Living Alone.* New York: The Penguin Press HC.

Kongtrül, D. (2006). *It's Up to You. The Practice of Self-Reflection on the Buddhist Path.* Boston: Shambhala Publications.

Kornfield, J., (2008). *The Wise Heart. A Guide to the Universal Teachings of Buddhist Psychology* (Abridged). Boulder, Colorado: Sounds True.

Kornfield, J. (1996). *The Inner Art of Meditation*. Boulder, Colorado: Sounds True. (VHS Video)

Korzybski, A. (1955). *Science and Sanity, 5th Edition.* Fort Worth, Texas: Institute of General Semantics.

Langer, E. (2009). *Counterclockwise. Mindful Health and the Power of Possibility.* New York: Ballantine Books.

Langer, E. (1989). *Mindfulness.* Reading, Massachusetts: Addison-Wesley Publishing Company, Inc.

LaRoche, L. (1995). *The Joy of STRESS.* Boston: WGBH. (VHS Video)

Lears, L. (2000). *Ben Has Something to Say: A Story About Stuttering.* Park Ridge, Illinois: Albert Whitman & Company.

Loori, J. D. (2008). *Bringing the Sacred to Life: The Daily Practice of Zen Ritual.* Boston: Shambhala Publications.

Macy, J. (1993). Schooling Our Intention. *Tricycle Magazine,* Vol. 3 (2) Winter.

Martin, W. (2005). *A Path and A Practice: Using Lao-Tzu's Tao Te Ching as a Path to Living a Spiritual Life.* Portland, Oregon: Marlowe & Company.

Mipham, S. (2012). *Running with the Mind of Meditation.* New York: Harmony.

Mipham, S. (2006). *Ruling Your World. Ancient Strategies for Modern Life.* New York: Three Rivers Press.

Moore, T. (2010). *Care of the Soul in Medicine. Healing Guidance for Patients, Families, and the People who Care for Them.* Carlsbad, California: Hay House.

Myss, C. (2009). The Mystical Approach to Healing Trauma. *Sounds True Holiday Catalogue,* p. 17.

Myss, C. (1998). *Why People Don't Heal and How They Can.* New York: Three Rivers Press.

Myss, C. (1997). *Why People Don't Heal and How They Can.* PBS. (VHS Video)

Neumann, R. (2012). *Not Quite Nirvana. A Skeptic's Guide to Mindfulness.* Berkeley, California: Parallax Press.

Norris, K. (2008). *Acedia & me. A Marriage, Monks, and a Writer's Life.* New York: Riverhead Books.

Orloff, J. (2005). *Positive Energy: 10 Extraordinary Prescripts for Transforming Fatigue, Stress, and Fear into Vibrance, Strength, and Love.* New York: Three Rivers Press.

Pagels, E. (1989). *The Gnostic Gospels.* New York, New York: Vintage Books.

REFERENCES

Piver, S. (2008). *Quiet Mind: A Beginner's Guide to Meditation.* Boston: Shambhala Publications.

Polsky, H. And Wozner, Y. (1989). *Everyday Miracles. The Healing Wisdom of Hasidic Stories.* New Jersey: Jason Aronson, Inc.

Rentschler, G., (2011) Covert Stuttering EXPOSED! Paper presented at the 14th annual ISAD International Online Conference, October.

Reynolds, D. (1980). *The Quiet Therapies: Japanese Pathways to Personal Growth.* Honolulu: University Press of Hawaii.

Reynolds, D. (1976). *Morita Psychotherapy.* Berkeley: University of California Press.

Rumi, J., Barks, C. and Moyne, J. (2004). *The Essential Rumi,* New Expanded Edition. New York: HarperOne.

Salt, J., & Murphy, R. (2010). *Eat Pray Love.* Screen adaptation of E. Gilbert (2007), *Eat Pray Love. One Woman's Search for Everything Across Italy, India and Indonesia.* New York: Penguin.

Salzberg, S. (2011). *Real Happiness. The Power of Meditation. A 28-Day Program.* New York: Workman Publishers. (Includes a CD)

Salzberg, S. (2004). *Lovingkindness Meditation.* Boulder, Colorado: Sounds True, Inc. (CD's)

Schacter-Shalomi, Z., (1997). *From Age-Ing to Sage-Ing: A Profound New Vision of Growing Older.* New York: Grand Central Publishing.

Scorsese, M. (2011). *Fran Lebowitz in "Public Speaking".* HBO Home Video.

Seligman, M., (2004). *Authentic Happiness. Utilizing the New Positive Psychology to Realize Your Potential for Lasting Fulfillment.* New York: Free Press.

Sheehan, J. (1958). Conflict Theory of Stuttering, pp. 121-166. In J. Eisenson (Ed.), *Stuttering: A Symposium*. New York: Harper & Row, Publishers, Inc.

Siegel, D. (2010). *Mindsight: The New Science of Personal Transformation*. New York: Bantam.

Silverman, E.-M. (2012c). Therapeutic Presence. *The ASHA Leader*, Vol. 17 (11), p. 2.

Silverman, E.-M. (2012b). Marginalizing Women. *The ASHA Leader*, Vol. 17 (4), p. 38.

Silverman, E.-M. (2012a). *Mindfulness & Stuttering. Using Eastern Strategies to Speak with Greater Ease*. North Charleston, South Carolina: CreateSpace Independent Publishing Platform.

Silverman, E.-M. (2011b). Self-Reflection in Clinical Practice, pp. 183-194. In R. Fourie (Ed.), *Therapeutic Processes for Communication Disorders*. London: Psychology Press.

Silverman, E.-M., (2011a). What to Expect from Mindfulness. Paper presented at the 14th Annual ISAD Online Conference, October.

Silverman, E.-M., (2009b). Doing the Work. Paper Presented at the 12th Annual ISAD Online Conference, October.

Silverman, E.-M. (2009a). *Mind Matters: Setting the Stage for Satisfying Clinical Service. A Personal Essay*. Charleston, South Carolina: BookSurge Publishing.

Silverman, E.-M. (2006b). Mind Matters. Presented at the 9th Annual ISAD Online Conference, October.

Silverman, E.-M. (2008a). Ongoing Self-Reflection. *American Journal of Speech-Language* Pathology,17, p. 92.

Silverman, E.-M., (2006a). A Personal Choice. *The ASHA Leader*, Vol. 11 (16), p. 47.

REFERENCES

Silverman, E.-M. (2005). *Jason's Secret: A Tool for Healing.* Unpublished manuscript.

Silverman, E.-M. (2005). *Shenpa,* Stuttering, and Me. Paper Presented at The 8th Annual ISAD Online Conference, October.

Silverman, E-M. (2003). My Personal Experience with Stuttering and Meditation.6th Annual ISAD Online Conference. October.

Silverman, E.-M. (2001). *Jason's Secret.* Bloomington, Indiana: 1st Books. Silverman, E.-M., (1986). The Female Stutterer, 35-63. In K. St. Louis (Ed.), *The Atypical Stutterer.* New York: Academic Press.

Silverman, E.-M. (1973). Clustering: A characteristic of preschoolers' speech disfluency. *J. Speech Hearing Res.,* 16, 578-583.

Silverman, E.-M., and Van Opens, K., (1980). An investigation of sex-bias in classroom teachers' speech and language referrals. *Language, Speech, and Hearing Services in the Schools,* 11, 169-174.

Silverman, E.-M., and Zimmer, C., (1979). Women who stutter: Personality and speech characteristics. *J. Speech Hearing Res.,* 22, 553-564.

Silverman, E.-M., and Zimmer, C., (1976). The fluency of women's speech, pp. 131-135. In I. Crouch and B. Dubois (Eds.), *Proceedings of the Conference on The Sociology of the Languages of American Women.* San Antonio: Trinity University.

Silverman, E.-M., and Zimmer, C., (1976). Replication of Speech fluency fluctuations during the menstrual cycle. *Percept. Mot. Skills,* 42, 1004-1006.

Silverman, E.-M., and Zimmer, C., (1975). Speech fluency fluctuations during the menstrual cycle. *J. Speech Hearing Res.,* 18, 202-206.

Silverman, E.-M., Zimmer, C., and Silverman, F., (1974). Variability in stutterers' speech disfluency: The menstrual cycle. *Percept. Mot. Skills*, 38, 1037-1038.

Silverman, E.-M., and Zimmer, C. (1982). Demographic characteristics and treatment experiences of women and men who stutter. *J. Fluency Dis.*, 7, 273-285.

Steiner, C. (1994). *Scripts People Live*. New York: Grove/Atlantic Press

Thernstrom, M. (2004). The Writing Cure. Can Understanding Narrative Make You a Better Doctor? *New York Times Magazine, April 18.*

Tolle, E., (2005). *A New Earth. Awakening to Your Life's Purpose*. New York: Penguin Group.

Turkle, S. (2012). *Alone Together. Why We Expect More from Technology and Less from Each Other*. New York: Basic Books.

von Franz, M.-L. (1964). "The Process of Individuation," pp. 158-230. In C.G. Jung, (Ed.), *Man and His Symbols*. New York: Doubleday.

Weil, A. (1995). *Spontaneous Healing*. New York: Alfred A. Knopf.

Whitney, M. (1986). *Matter of Heart. The Extraordinary Journey of C. G. Jung Into the Soul of Man*. New York: Kino International Corp. (DVD)

Williams, D.E. (1957). A point of view about 'stuttering. *Journal of Speech & Hearing Disorders, 22,* 3, 390-397.

Winston, D. (2010). Saying Yes to an Open Heart, pp. 31-32. *Buddhadharma: The Practitioner's Quarterly*, Summer.

Woollams, S. & Brown, M. (1979). *TA: The Total Handbook of Transactional Analysis*. Englewood Cliffs, N.J.: Prentice-Hall, Inc.

ACKNOWLEDGEMENTS

This compilation of conference papers plus commentary on each written especially for this book presents knowledge distilled from decades of experience learning to live lightly as someone whose stuttering problem once impaired her ability to communicate and whose propensity for blaming helped forestall her healing. As I reflect on what I know and what I recall of the process, I recognize I have benefitted from all my experience, even that which brought considerable pain at first. Each contact with an individual or individuals and each experience whether through seemingly random happenstance or through formalized arrangement of one sort or another taught me something about myself or about others that prepared me to speak and live with greater ease.

Naming them all here, even if I knew and remembered their names, would be impractical and, probably, as unnecessary as it occasionally would be surprising. Some of the most transformative exchanges have been brief, fleeting, or singular, such as a warm smile offered by a stranger seated beside me in an airplane whose temporary, engaging fellowship served as a potent reminder that life offers more than we customarily think. And some have been with those acting as enemies or *frenemies* who delivered taunts, jibes, and slights or engaged in betrayal with the intent to waylay me that, instead, ultimately sparked the discovery of capacities and the development of skills to relate to anger and hurt in ways that strengthened me.

But I want to acknowledge one person whose vision helped launch this particular enterprise, Eric Berne, M.D. The late Eric

Berne, founder of transactional analysis, a psychiatrist and clinical observer I never met personally, encouraged me through his writing to communicate with the general reader, not just professionals. He believed that if people knew what professionals knew about the importance of communicating more effectively with themselves and practical ways to do so, they could change to be more as they wished without necessarily enrolling in extensive and, often, expensive therapy programs and services or purchasing costly equipment and materials. Although I came to realize that clinicians before him also wrote for the public with the same intent, for instance, psychoanalysts Carl Jung and Marie-Louise von Franz and psychiatrist and *logopedist* Viktor Frankl, and I know many have since, it was Dr. Berne's expression of this potent aspect of the clinician's role that I encountered first. I remain especially grateful to him for opening my eyes to this possibility for a clinician and a researcher to be helpful.

Although, based on merit, I am unqualified to stand alongside this exemplar, his mission has become mine as well. If you find the information in this book useful, Eric Berne deserves your appreciation. His vision helped motivate and prepare me to write it.

ABOUT THE AUTHOR

Ellen-Marie Silverman was director of the Fluency Clinic while a tenured faculty member at Marquette University. She holds the Ph.D. in speech pathology from the University of Iowa and was a post-doctoral fellow in developmental psycholinguistics at The University of Illinois, Urbana-Champaign. Later, she trained to be a transactional analysis counselor. A clinical and research speech-language pathologist and Fellow of the American Speech-Hearing-Language Association, she has provided direction and support to people with stuttering problems for more than 40 years.

She has presented nationally and internationally to colleagues and students about the nature, prevention, and treatment of stuttering problems. The recipient of research awards, Ellen-Marie Silverman has published extensively in peer-reviewed publications, contributed chapters to textbooks, and authored the clinical text, *Mind Matters. Setting the Stage for Satisfying Clinical Service. A Personal Essay.* She wrote *Jason's Secret,* a novel for readers from 9 to 12, about a 10 year-old boy taking his first steps to constructively resolve his stuttering problem to illustrate what a stuttering problem can feel like to a child and the straight-forward steps caring adults can take to help. And, in the breakthrough book, *Mindfulness & Stuttering. Using Eastern Strategies to Speak with Greater Ease,* she drew from her more than 16-year experimentation and experience with six mindfulness techniques –- *shamatha-vipassana*, working with *shenpa, maitri, lojong*, reciting *gatha's*, and *tonglen* –- to addresses questions and concerns people may have about the practice of mindfulness and its application to stuttering problems.

Dr. Silverman has been a member of the faculties of Marquette University, The University of Illinois at Urbana-Champaign, and The Medical College of Wisconsin. Most recently, she has been CEO of TSS, Inc., a healthcare staffing support service she founded and operated through which she helped pioneer open captioning for live theater.

An artist, Ellen-Marie Silverman's paintings, drawings, and installations have been included in various juried art shows.

Made in the USA
Middletown, DE
15 October 2018